once upon a chef, the cookbook

once upon a chef

THE COOKBOOK

100 TESTED, PERFECTED, *and* FAMILY-APPROVED RECIPES

JENNIFER SEGAL

photographs by ALEXANDRA GRABLEWSKI

CHRONICLE BOOKS

SAN FRANCISCO

Library of Congress Cataloging-in-Publication Data

Names: Segal, Jennifer, author.
Title: Once upon a chef, the cookbook : 100 tested,
   perfected, and family-approved recipes / Jennifer Segal.
Description: San Francisco : Chronicle Books, [2018] |
   Includes index.
Identifiers: LCCN 2017005019 | ISBN 9781452156187
   (hc : alk. paper)
Subjects: LCSH: Cooking—Technique. | Cooking. |
   LCGFT: Cookbooks.
Classification: LCC TX651 .S424 2018 | DDC 641.5—dc23 LC
record available at https://lccn.loc.gov/2017005019

Manufactured in China.

Photographs by Alexandra Grablewski
Prop Styling by Maeve Sheridan
Food Styling by Cyd McDowell

Design by Alice Chau
Typesetting by Frank Brayton

10 9 8 7 6 5 4 3 2 1

Chronicle books and gifts are available at special quantity
discounts to corporations, professional associations, literacy
programs, and other organizations. For details and discount
information, please contact our premiums department at
corporatesales@chroniclebooks.com or at 1-800-759-0190.

Chronicle Books LLC
680 Second Street
San Francisco, California 94107
www.chroniclebooks.com

To Mom & Dad, for always encouraging me to chase my dreams, especially this one.

To my wonderful agent, Maria Ribas, who discovered my blog a few years ago and asked if I was still interested in writing a cookbook. Thank you for ushering this book from idea to reality, and for being my coach, friend, and cheerleader along the way. You are amazing.

To my small but mighty Once Upon a Chef team: Lacy Walpert, for your endless creativity and positive attitude—and for pushing me outside my comfort zone (yes, good things do happen). And Betsy Goldstein, my do-everything colleague, whose attention to detail, wit, and work ethic are second to none; I don't know how I managed before you came on board. I love working with you both.

To my editors, Amy Treadwell and Sarah Billingsley, for believing in this book and making it so much better than it was. Thank you for taking a chance on a first-time author and guiding me through the process. To Alice Chau and the entire Chronicle Books team: I'm honored to be part of your beautiful cookbook tradition.

To the lovely Alexandra Grablewski for her gorgeous photography and impeccable eye. To Cyd McDowell, Christine Buckley, and Brett Regot for their boundless energy and flawless food styling. And to Maeve Sheridan for supplying the fabulous props that brought the photos and recipes to life.

To my mom, who always taught me to work hard and believe in my aspirations, no matter how far-fetched they seemed. Thank you for being my biggest champion—and for proofreading my blog posts all these years, even when you had way more important things to do.

A heartfelt thank you to my dad, who pored over every word of my manuscript with a red pen before I submitted it to my editor, although he never cooked a day in his life. Dad, can you believe you're still helping me with my homework?

To my sister, Erica, for encouraging me to start a cooking blog, when I had no clue what a blog was. And for patiently answering a million "Which do you like better?" text messages about the design of this book.

To my husband Michael for giving me the runway to follow my dreams—and for being the kind of dad that allowed me to dive into this project without worrying for one second about the kids. Thank you for never complaining about eating the same dinner five nights in a row while I tried to get it right.

To my kids, Zach and Anna, for understanding my long nights at the computer—and for laughing when I forgot to pick you up from practice, complete the fieldtrip form, or fill in the blank. You guys have been on my hip or by my side from the start. I feel like we created this book together.

Finally, to all of my blog readers: thank you for bringing me into your kitchens and giving me the opportunity to do what I love every day. Without your support, this book would simply not exist.

contents

introduction

THE FIRST FLICKER of an idea for this cookbook came to me about twenty years ago when I was working my first kitchen job at L'Auberge Chez François, an acclaimed French restaurant tucked into the rolling hills of Virginia, right outside of Washington, D.C. It was late at night after a grueling shift, and I had a nasty burn on my wrist to show for it. Fighting back tears, I wiped down my station and thought to myself, "What on earth have I gotten myself into?" The restaurant had a large, European-style brigade kitchen with the chef at the helm and all the cooks "manning" their stations. Not only was I the only woman, at five feet two inches tall, I was also hopelessly undersized for the massive equipment that surrounded us. I had to get lifts on my shoes just to reach the plates over the stove—and don't even ask about those fifty-pound sacks of potatoes!

My job as the newbie in the L'Auberge kitchen was to prepare all of the vegetables during the day, and then operate two large deck ovens that kept plates and vegetables warm during the dinner service. Every time an order came in, I arranged the appropriate vegetables on a plate, covered the plate with an aluminum pie pan, and stacked it in the oven with dozens of others. When the chef

called the order for pickup, I located the piping hot plate in the oven and handed it off to the more experienced cooks to add the entrée. I did this same job every night for an entire year. To this day, my dad teases me that he paid for four years of college and culinary school so that I could be a professional plate warmer.

The truth is that even though I went to culinary school and graduated with honors, I was completely overwhelmed with what I was doing. No amount of schooling or passion for cooking can prepare you for the rigors of working in a restaurant kitchen: juggling an incessant stream of orders, sweltering heat, flames, short tempers, sharp knives—it was terrifying! Thankfully, my fellow cooks took me under their wings, jumping over to my station to pitch in if I got in the weeds or covering for me if I screwed up. I *loved* those guys. Eventually, I got the hang of it, but I knew from the start that I was not cut out for an adrenaline-charged career as a restaurant chef. Instead, I wondered, "Maybe I could write a cookbook?"

Fast-forward about five years and a few restaurant jobs later: I met Michael and we got married, and had our son, Zach, two years later. I happily left the restaurant business to be a stay-at-home mom, and then my daughter, Anna, was born seventeen months later. With two little ones, I had my hands full—literally! When Anna started preschool, though, I got the itch to go back to work and start cooking more than just buttered noodles and chicken nuggets.

One day, a girlfriend of mine asked me to bake a cake for her son's fourth birthday party. I spent three days baking and decorating a three-tier farm-themed cake with blue and green fondant icing and handmade barnyard animal cookies grazing around the edges of each layer. Granted, I went a little (okay, a lot) overboard, but it was so much fun, I decided to start a business baking specialty cakes and cupcakes, mostly for children's birthday parties. Through developing my cake recipes, I realized how much I loved the process of creating, testing, and perfecting recipes, so I started to think about ways I could turn that into a career. What about that cookbook?

I knew that getting published as an unknown was a long shot, so, at the advice of my younger (and hipper) sister, Erica, I decided in 2009 to start a food blog instead. I came up with the name Once Upon a Chef, registered my domain, and began creating and posting recipes every week. Little by little, my readership grew from one—my mom—to a millions-strong following from all over the world. I had finally found my dream job: one that allowed me to cook restaurant-level food every day without sweating it out nights and weekends in a professional kitchen. And thanks to the loyalty and support of my readers, the blog ultimately led to the opportunity to fulfill my longtime dream of writing a cookbook.

Over the years, I've gotten to know my readers—teenagers and newlyweds learning to cook, young mothers making their child's first birthday cake, working parents looking for solutions to the "What's for dinner?" dilemma, grandmothers cooking for their extended families, singles and couples who cook for themselves, and retirees taking up cooking as a hobby. And I feel so honored to be a part of my readers' lives through my recipes.

I also feel a great deal of responsibility to make sure the recipes are foolproof. That's why, from the start, I decided to be 100 percent committed to testing and perfecting my recipes. I know how much time and effort goes into shopping for and cooking a meal, and, as a busy mom of two young teens myself, I know there is precious little time to waste on bad recipes. So for me, a recipe can't just be good—it has to be good enough to write home about. It has to be that slam-dunk recipe that you just can't wait to make again and again. The fact is, cooking is fun and gratifying when recipes are simple to execute and as delicious as promised. But it's downright frustrating when the process is confusing or the results disappointing.

Just like on my blog, I have tested every recipe in this book extensively in my home kitchen. But you don't have to take my word alone that the recipes work. When I announced on my blog that I was writing a cookbook, I was inundated with volunteers for recipe testers. So the recipes have been tested by hundreds of home cooks just like you. Thanks to my recipe testers' feedback, I was able to tweak recipes that needed adjustments, anticipate any potential questions, and even eliminate a few recipes that weren't home runs.

My hope is that when you flip through the chapters of this book, you'll want to dog-ear every page—whether it's an easy weeknight dinner your family will love, a birthday cake for your special someone, granola bars to pack in the kids' lunches, or a fun cocktail to make when the neighbors drop by on Friday night. And I hope that with each recipe completed, you'll feel more confident in the kitchen. Remember, I'm right there with you—and just an e-mail away if you ever have any questions, feedback, or even a recipe of your own that you'd like to share. Please drop me a line through my website. I'd love to hear from you!

Jenn

welcome to my kitchen!

I LIVE ONLY A STONE'S THROW from the bustle of Washington, D.C., but it truly feels like the country here, with winding roads, horse barns, and even the occasional wild turkey strutting around the backyard. If you were to come visit on any given evening, you'd walk through the foyer and then directly into our kitchen, the center of our home both literally and figuratively. I'd be at the stove cooking dinner with our sweet labrador, Miles, underfoot; the kids would be doing homework (and annoying each other) at the kitchen table; and my husband, Michael, would be milling around, looking for something to eat.

It's universally true, isn't it? No matter how many other rooms in the house, everyone gravitates to the kitchen. I remember when my kids were little, while I made dinner, they used to chase each other round and round the kitchen island, which drove me crazy. Now they bounce basketballs around it, which drives me even more crazy! And even though my desk is in the living room, I always set my laptop on the breakfast

table, where there's cheerful sunlight streaming in, tea on demand, and a view of the garden.

We designed our kitchen when we were young, so it's far from perfect. I pine every day for a walk-in pantry and dual wall ovens, but overall it functions well, with a good work triangle, a broad farm sink, and a large center island great for prepping (and also, regrettably, for collecting junk mail, backpacks, and other random stuff).

When it comes to stocking the kitchen, I'm pretty practical. I don't believe in buying every conceivable kitchen gadget, but do believe you need a good arsenal; otherwise cooking can be tedious. And it's important to keep your most essential kitchen tools and appliances within easy reach, or else you'll never want to use them. I keep my most-used pots, pans, and colanders hanging from a pot rack over the kitchen island. And my food processor, heavy-duty mixer, and blender live right on the countertop, workspace be damned. If I had to hoist heavy equipment up from underneath a cabinet, I'd avoid all recipes that required me to use it.

The list that follows is not intended to be compulsory—everyone most certainly has different space limitations and budgets. But I thought it'd be helpful to share the kitchen tools and appliances I use most often, and especially for the recipes in this book.

KNIVES

Some people have their favorite pens—my husband has used the same pen to sign every important document since before we were married—but I have my favorite knives. I reach for the same ones again and again, which goes to show that you really only need a few: a bread knife, a chef's knife, a paring knife, and a serrated utility knife. Good knives last forever; in fact, I've had mine so long that they have my maiden name engraved on them!

KNIFE SHARPENER

It's counterintuitive, but you're much less likely to cut yourself with a sharp knife than a dull one. Sharp knives grip food better, so the edge doesn't slip. I use an electric knife sharpener to sharpen my knives regularly, but a honing steel or manual handheld sharpener works well, too.

CUTTING BOARDS

I use several cutting boards when I'm cooking to avoid cross-contamination of raw proteins and cooked foods, as well as cross-contamination of flavors. There's nothing worse than biting into a sliced apple and tasting raw onions. As much as I love the look and feel of wooden cutting boards, they're heavy and a pain to clean and maintain. So I tend to reach for my plastic ones, which are light, durable, and dishwasher-safe.

POTS AND PANS

One of the most common questions I field every day is: "What pots and pans do you recommend?" I always suggest a good set of stainless-steel pots and pans as your everyday workhorses. And get the best ones you can afford; they'll perform better and be easier to clean. Every kitchen also needs at least two nonstick sauté pans (an 8-in [20-cm] and a 10-in [25-cm]) and a large roasting pan with a rack. If there's room in the budget for one more, a Dutch oven (with at least a 6-qt [6-L] capacity) is a worthwhile investment. The stainless-steel pans and Dutch oven will last forever, but nonstick pans should be replaced as soon as they get worn.

HEAVY-DUTY MIXER

I have a heavy-duty KitchenAid mixer that I swear by. It was once working so hard kneading dough that it inched off the countertop and fell on the floor—and it still works! An electric hand mixer will work too, but keep in mind that it's not as powerful, so mixing times may need to be increased.

FOOD PROCESSOR

I find most people get a food processor as a wedding or housewarming gift and then it lives in the basement or a hard-to-reach cabinet in the kitchen and never gets used. I leave mine right on the countertop and use it almost daily to mix dough, grate cheese, chop vegetables, purée dips, and more. I even use it to make my No-Churn Cheesecake Ice Cream (page 242) and chocolate frosting (see page 275). All of the pieces go right into the dishwasher, so it's easy to clean. Get one with at least an 11-cup [2.6-L] capacity if possible. And don't try to purée liquids in it (that's what a blender is for); any liquid over the top of the blade will leak out and make a huge mess.

STANDARD BLENDER

This is another appliance I keep right on the countertop for making smoothies, milk shakes, frozen drinks, and salad dressings. While a high-performance blender, such as the Vitamix, is great for making ultrasmooth soups, juices, and smoothies that don't need to be strained, it's not essential.

IMMERSION BLENDER

Puréeing hot soup in multiple batches in a blender—not to mention the multiple bowls and pots it requires—is a pain in the neck. So I'm a big fan of my handheld immersion blender. You simply immerse the blender into the pot, press the "on" button, and circle it around. Plus, it's inexpensive, easy to clean, and takes up very little space.

STAINLESS-STEEL OR GLASS NESTING BOWLS

A set of three or more stainless-steel or glass mixing bowls that stack inside one another is a cooking staple, and also a space saver.

SHEET PANS

Every kitchen needs a few good rimmed baking sheets (also called half-sheet pans, cookie sheets, or jelly-roll pans) for baking cookies, roasting vegetables, and even transporting food around the kitchen or to and from the grill. The standard size is 13-by-18 in [33-by-46 cm]. Be sure to buy heavy, good-quality pans so they won't buckle in the oven under high heat.

BAKING DISHES

I've accumulated quite a collection of baking dishes (I can't resist a pretty one!), but the only ones you really need are a 9-by-13-in [23-by-33-cm] pan, an

8-in [20-cm] square pan, a 9-in [23-cm] square pan, and a few smaller (1- to 2-qt [1- to 2-L] capacity) oven-to-table baking dishes. If you're a baker, you'll also need two 8- or 9-in [20- or 23-cm] round cake pans and at least one 9-by-1½-in [23-by-4-cm] pie pan.

COLANDERS AND STRAINERS

A large colander with a footed base is a must for draining pasta. I also have a set of fine-mesh sieves in different sizes—large ones for straining soups and sauces, and small ones for sifting cocoa powder or powdered sugar over desserts.

A DIGITAL KITCHEN SCALE

I recently started including weight measurements in my recipes for my readers outside the United States, and now I'm a convert. The fact is: volumetric measurements are inaccurate for anything except liquids. Think about three cups of broccoli florets and how much that measurement can vary depending on how the broccoli is cut and packed into the measuring cup. A digital scale takes much of the guesswork out of cooking—plus, it's inexpensive, easy to use, and small.

DRY AND LIQUID MEASURING CUPS

The first step to measuring correctly is to start with the right measuring tools (see above). You need at least one set of measuring spoons and two sets of measuring cups: one for measuring dry ingredients and one for measuring liquids. Dry measuring cups are designed to be filled up to the top and then leveled off with a straight edge. Liquid

measuring cups have a pour spout and are filled to the gradations on the side of the cup.

CITRUS JUICER

If you've ever made my Persian Lime "Key Lime" Pie (page 247) or Luscious Lemon Squares (page 263), you know why you need a citrus juicer: juicing more than a few citrus fruits by hand is downright tedious. I actually prefer the inexpensive manual juicers to the fancy electric ones, as they take up less space.

BOX GRATER AND RASP GRATER

A box grater with coarse and fine grating surfaces as well as a slicing blade is a must-have kitchen tool. I also highly recommend a rasp grater, a long, skinny tool that works well for zesting citrus peel and grating hard cheeses.

UTENSILS

Every kitchen needs a battery of utensils: whisks; wooden spoons; slotted spoons; a vegetable peeler; a garlic press; rubber, metal, and offset spatulas; tongs; kitchen shears; and ladles.

COOKING THERMOMETERS

An instant-read thermometer and leave-in thermometer are both essential for making sure meat and poultry are properly and safely cooked (see page 153 for how to tell when meat is done). If you're interested in deep-frying or making confections, a candy thermometer is a must, too, since instant-read thermometer temperature ranges don't go high enough for tasks like boiling sugar or oil.

starters & snacks

The line between what constitutes a starter versus a main course is happily blurry for me. I love to dine out with Michael and order a bottle of wine and a spread of appetizers as our meal. The starters are often the most interesting dishes on the menu, and I'm hopelessly indecisive (and greedy) when it comes to good food. Why settle on one dish when you can sample and share several?

I also love hosting appetizer-only get-togethers at home. Friends relaxing on the patio in comfy chairs, festive cocktails, an assortment of fun, tasty bites—now that's a party I want to be at! It's also one I enjoy throwing: even if I'm cooking the same amount of food in the end, somehow it feels less overwhelming than preparing a traditional meal.

The recipes in this chapter are a mix of flavorful snacks and nibbles, creamy dips, and dishes substantial enough to serve as a light supper. Of course, the question with starters is always how much to make. I have an irrational fear of running out of food and always make way too much. But the general rule is: If starters will be followed by a meal, serve two to three different options, each with at least two servings per guest; and if the party is timed so that the small plates are meant to be dinner, serve four to five different things, each with at least three servings per person.

Lastly, if you're going to a party instead of throwing one, you'll find many make-ahead dishes in this chapter that travel well, and a few of them—like the Sweet, Salty, Spicy Pecans (page 21) and Joanne's Refrigerator Dill Pickles (page 25)—also make lovely hostess gifts.

sweet, salty, spicy pecans

THESE NUTS ARE MADLY ADDICTIVE. They're perfect to serve with cocktails, toss over salads, or just keep around the house over the holidays. They also make a delicious homemade gift. The best part? You only need four simple ingredients to make them—and, if you start right now, you'll be done in 15 minutes. Makes 2 cups [280 g]

½ cup [60 g] confectioners' sugar

¾ tsp kosher salt

½ tsp cayenne pepper

2 cups [225 g] whole pecans

sourcing savvy

Other nuts may be substituted, but pecans work best here—the coating sinks into all the crevices, making them deliciously crisp and flavorful.

1. Preheat the oven to 350°F [180°C] and set an oven rack in the middle position. Line a rimmed 13-by-18-in [33-by-46-cm] baking sheet with parchment paper.

2. In a medium bowl, whisk together the confectioners' sugar, salt, and cayenne.

3. Add the pecans to the sugar mixture, along with 4 teaspoons of water. Stir until the sugar is dissolved into a sticky glaze and all the nuts are evenly coated. (If the mixture is still too powdery after stirring for a while, it's okay to add a few more drops of water—just don't add too much.)

4. Transfer the pecans to the prepared baking sheet and arrange in a single layer. Scrape every last bit of glaze from the bowl and drizzle over the nuts. Bake for 10 to 12 minutes, until the pecans are crusty on top and caramelized and golden on the bottom. Immediately slide the parchment off of the hot baking sheet and allow the pecans to cool completely on the countertop. Once cool, remove the pecans from the parchment, breaking apart any clusters if necessary, and store in an airtight container at room temperature for up to 2 weeks. (Do not freeze.)

buttery cajun-spiced popcorn

I CONFESS: When home alone, I'm happy to forgo dinner so long as I have a generous supply of popcorn. Yes, popcorn-as-a-meal while binge-watching Netflix is my idea of a fun night in. And since popcorn is basically a blank slate just waiting for interesting flavors, why settle for just butter and salt? With a sprinkling of Cajun spices, you've got an instant upgrade and perfect party eat.

This recipe is meant to serve four, but two could just as easily share it. One of my recipe testers actually wrote: "It's only enough for one—ME!" Serves 4

sourcing savvy

Microwave popcorn is marketed as more convenient than stovetop popcorn, but the truth is that making homemade stovetop popcorn is hardly any more difficult. There are literally only two steps: heat the oil and kernels in a pot and pop. And no unfamiliar additives!

pro tip

When popping homemade popcorn, be sure to use the right-sized pot. The kernels need to be in a single layer to ensure even popping. (If you'd like to double the recipe, use two pots.) And don't skimp on the oil or the kernels will pop unevenly and burn.

3 Tbsp vegetable oil	¾ tsp salt
⅔ cup [140 g] popcorn kernels	½ tsp onion powder
5 Tbsp [70 g] unsalted butter	¼ tsp sugar
1½ tsp paprika	¼ tsp cayenne pepper
1 tsp garlic powder	

1. Pour the vegetable oil into a large (8-qt [8-L]) pot over medium-high heat. Add the popcorn kernels, then cover.

2. Wait for the popcorn to start popping, then shake the pan gently every 15 seconds to keep the kernels moving. When the popping slows to 2 to 3 seconds apart, remove the pan from the heat. Transfer the popcorn to a large bowl for mixing.

3. Melt the butter in a small saucepan or in a small bowl in the microwave. In another small bowl, whisk together the paprika, garlic powder, salt, onion powder, sugar, and cayenne. Drizzle a third of the butter over the popcorn. Sprinkle with a third of the spice mix; toss well. Drizzle another third of the butter over the popcorn and sprinkle with another third of the spice mix; toss well. Repeat with the remaining butter and spice mix. Toss well until the popcorn is evenly coated. Serve warm or at room temperature.

joanne's refrigerator dill pickles

THE KIDS AND I DISCOVERED a jar of these pickles in my parents' refrigerator door one day and since then, no deli or store-bought pickles have ever come close. They were made by one of my mom's oldest and dearest friends, Joanne Biltekoff, a remarkable lady both in and out of the kitchen.

The best thing about Joanne's pickles is that they're quick and easy— no sterilizing jars or special canning equipment required. All you do is slice Kirby cucumbers into spears, cover them with brine, tuck them into the fridge, and they're ready to eat the next day. Makes about 24 spears, or two 1-qt [1-L] jars

1¼ cups [300 ml] distilled white vinegar (5 percent acidity)

3 Tbsp kosher salt

2 Tbsp sugar

2 cups [480 ml] cold water

1¾ to 2 lb [800 to 900 g] Kirby cucumbers, cut into halves or spears

2 Tbsp coriander seeds

6 large garlic cloves, halved

1 tsp mustard seeds

¼ tsp crushed red pepper flakes

16 fresh dill sprigs

sourcing savvy

The most important part of this recipe is to start with Kirby, or pickling, cucumbers. They're short, squat, and not that pretty, but they make deliciously crisp pickles. Don't be tempted to substitute another variety or you'll end up with soggy pickles.

pro tip

When cooking high-acid foods, be sure to use a cooking vessel made from a nonreactive material such as stainless steel, glass, ceramic, or Teflon. Pots made from metals like aluminum, copper, or cast iron will react with the acid and give your food a metallic taste.

1. Combine the vinegar, salt, and sugar in a small nonreactive saucepan (see Pro Tip) over high heat. Whisk until the salt and sugar are dissolved. Transfer the liquid to a bowl and whisk in the water. Refrigerate the brine until cool or ready to use.

2. Tightly pack the cucumbers lengthwise into two clean 1-qt [1-L] jars. Add the coriander seeds, garlic cloves, mustard seeds, red pepper flakes, dill sprigs, and chilled brine to the jars, dividing evenly. If necessary, add a bit of cold water to the jars until the brine covers the cucumbers. Cover and refrigerate for at least 24 hours before serving. The pickles will keep in the refrigerator for up to 1 month.

homemade tortilla chips

serve with chunky pea guacamole with roasted jalapeños (PAGE 28).

(PAGE 28)

heads up

Depending on how long you cook the chips, they'll either be slightly soft in the center or crisp all over. Personally, I love the ones that are crisp and golden around the edges but still a little pale and bendy in the middle.

WHETHER I'M MAKING Baja Fish Tacos (page 117) or Chicken Tortilla Soup (page 65), I always seem to end up with a huge stack of leftover corn tortillas. Why they come so many to a pack is beyond me, but I've solved the dilemma with this homemade tortilla chip recipe. The only problem is that once you try them, it's hard to go back to the store-bought kind. Serves 4

1½ cups [360 ml] vegetable oil	½ tsp salt
Eight 6-in [15-cm] corn tortillas, cut into quarters	¼ tsp ground cumin

1. Pour the oil into a medium skillet to a depth of about ¼ in [6 mm].

2. Heat the oil over medium-high heat until a tortilla triangle placed in the oil sizzles.

3. Line a baking sheet with paper towels. Place a handful of tortilla triangles in the hot oil in a single layer. Fry for about 30 seconds, then use tongs or a slotted spoon to flip the chips. Continue frying for 30 to 45 seconds more, until the chips are crisp and golden brown. You might have to adjust the heat of the oil as you go. If the chips are browning too quickly, lower the heat; if they're cooking too slowly, increase the heat.

4. Continue to fry the chips, working in batches and putting the freshly fried chips on a new layer of paper towel each time. Sprinkle each batch with salt and cumin while still warm and toss to coat. Serve immediately.

chunky pea guacamole with roasted jalapeños

serve with homemade tortilla chips (PAGE 26).

THIS IS THE RECIPE that caused an uproar in the media a few years ago, when the *New York Times* tweeted a guacamole recipe with the caption, "Add peas to your guacamole. Trust us." People were outraged by the idea of messing with such a classic recipe. But I thought, "How bad could it be?" Sure enough, it was delicious. The peas add an appealing sweetness and chunkiness to the dip and also intensify the green color. I should note that the original recipe in the *Times* (from ABC Cocina in New York City) calls for garnishing the guacamole with some of the peas and also sunflower seeds. I think the peas look weird on top, so I just mix them all in. And as for the sunflower seeds, I leave them out—that's where I draw the line! Serves 6

2 small jalapeño peppers

⅔ cup [85 g] thawed frozen or cooked fresh peas

2 Tbsp chopped fresh cilantro, plus more for garnish

3 ripe avocados, peeled, pitted, and diced

3 scallions, white and light green parts only, thinly sliced

Zest of 1 lime

Juice of 1 lime (about 2 Tbsp), plus more as needed

¾ tsp salt

Tortilla chips, for serving

Lime wedges, for serving (optional)

pro tip

Most of the heat in a jalapeño pepper is in the ribs and seeds, so for a spicier guacamole, go ahead and add some of the seeds.

1. Heat the broiler to high and set an oven rack in the top position. Line a small baking pan with heavy-duty aluminum foil.

2. Place one of the jalapeños on the prepared pan and broil, turning occasionally, until the pepper is completely charred, a few minutes. (Alternatively, if you have a gas stove, turn a burner to the highest setting and, using a pair of tongs, set your pepper directly on the flame. Use the tongs to turn the pepper until the skin is completely blackened.) Immediately place the blackened pepper in a small bowl, cover it tightly with plastic wrap, and let it steam for 15 minutes. When the pepper is cool enough to handle, use a paper towel to wipe off the charred skin. Halve, seed, and dice the roasted jalapeño. Then halve, seed, and dice the remaining raw jalapeño.

3. In the bowl of a food processor fitted with the steel blade, combine the peas with the roasted jalapeño, raw jalapeño, and cilantro. Process to a coarse purée. (Alternatively, you can finely chop the mixture with a knife.)

4. In a medium bowl, combine the avocados, scallions, lime zest and juice, salt, and pea-jalapeño purée. Mash until well combined but still a little chunky. Taste and adjust the salt and lime juice as needed. Serve with tortilla chips and lime wedges, if desired.

MAKE AHEAD: Guacamole should always be made as fresh as possible, but to keep it from turning brown, press a piece of plastic wrap directly over the top and store in the refrigerator until ready to serve.

l'auberge chez françois
herbed cottage cheese spread

serve with garlic & herb ciabatta (PAGE 237) or crackers.

MY FIRST JOB OUT OF CULINARY SCHOOL was as an apprentice to Chef Jacques Haeringer at L'Auberge Chez François, a renowned French restaurant in Great Falls, Virginia, a picturesque suburb of Washington, D.C. It was a thrill to be a part of the team, especially since I had grown up dining there with my family on special occasions.

One of the nicest parts about dinner at Chez François is all the unexpected treats that show up at your table throughout the meal, like decadent chocolate truffles after dessert, sorbets garnished with candied violets between courses—or, my personal favorite, the Herbed Cottage Cheese Spread that comes with a basket of toasted garlic bread while you peruse the menu. It's the perfect beginning to an always-perfect meal. Thank you, Chef Jacques, for sharing the recipe. Serves 6 to 8

1 lb [455 g] 4 percent milk fat small-curd, cream-style cottage cheese

⅔ cup [160 g] sour cream

1 Tbsp finely minced shallot

1 Tbsp finely minced scallions or fresh chives, plus more for garnish

1 Tbsp finely minced fresh Italian parsley, plus more for garnish

1 tsp finely minced garlic

½ tsp salt

¼ tsp freshly ground black pepper

sourcing savvy

For best results, do not use low-fat cottage cheese or sour cream.

1. Combine the cottage cheese and sour cream in a medium bowl and blend well. Add the remaining ingredients. Mix thoroughly and adjust the seasoning, if necessary. Cover and refrigerate until ready to serve. Garnish with parsley and chives before serving.

MAKE AHEAD: This dip can be made up to 2 days ahead of time and stored in an airtight container in the refrigerator.

roasted eggplant & chickpea tapenade

IF YOU'RE A CAPONATA or tapenade lover like me, you'll love this chunky Mediterranean-style dip. I like to serve it as part of a spread of appetizers with hummus and pita chips—because honestly, as much as I love hummus, it's become so ubiquitous that I've gotten a little bored with it. It's nice to mix it up! This recipe makes a ton; leftovers are wonderful spread on toasted pita for lunch. Serves 6 to 8

sourcing savvy

There are many different varieties of eggplant. For this recipe, use the regular globe eggplant, which is the variety you're most likely to find at the supermarket. It will have a deep purple color, a long and elongated oval shape, and smooth skin.

5 Tbsp [80 ml] extra-virgin olive oil

One 1-lb [455-g] eggplant, peeled and sliced into ½-in [12-mm] rounds

3 large garlic cloves

Salt

One 15½-oz [445-g] can chickpeas, drained and rinsed

¾ cup [110 g] jarred pimento-stuffed green olives, drained

½ cup [115 g] chopped roasted red peppers from a jar, drained

½ cup [10 g] loosely packed fresh Italian parsley leaves, roughly chopped

1 Tbsp finely chopped fresh thyme, plus a few small sprigs for serving (optional)

1 tsp ground cumin

¼ tsp cayenne pepper

Store-bought pita chips for serving

1. Preheat the oven to 350°F [180°C] and set an oven rack in the middle position. Line a rimmed 13-by-18-in [33-by-46-cm] baking sheet with heavy-duty aluminum foil.

2. Drizzle 1½ tablespoons of the oil on the prepared baking sheet and spread around with your hands. Place the eggplant rounds and garlic on the foil. Then drizzle with another 1½ tablespoons of the olive oil and sprinkle with ½ teaspoon of salt. Roast for 20 minutes.

3. Transfer the roasted eggplant and garlic to the bowl of a food processor fitted with the steel blade. Pulse until finely chopped (it will look a little mashed), and then transfer to a large bowl.

4. Add the chickpeas to the bowl of the food processor (no need to wash it beforehand). Pulse until just chunky, and then add to the bowl with the eggplant mixture. Add the olives, red peppers, and parsley to the bowl of the food processor and pulse until coarsely chopped. Transfer to the bowl with the eggplant and chickpeas.

5. Stir the remaining 2 tablespoons olive oil, the 1 tablespoon thyme, the cumin, ¾ teaspoon salt, and the cayenne into the tapenade. Taste and adjust the seasoning, if necessary. If possible, refrigerate for at least 30 minutes to allow the flavors to marry.

6. Transfer the spread to a serving bowl and sprinkle with the thyme sprigs, if desired. Serve with the pita chips.

MAKE AHEAD: This dip can be made up to 2 days ahead of time and stored in an airtight container in the refrigerator.

warm caramelized onion & gruyère dip

CARAMELIZING ONIONS TAKES PATIENCE. There's no cheating it: the onions need to be cooked low and slow so that they turn a rich caramel color without a touch of burning (see photo). But the payoff in flavor is well worth the time. This appetizer is like French onion soup in dip form. It's rich, rich, rich—save it for a special occasion or friends with hearty appetites. Serves 6 to 8

3 Tbsp unsalted butter

6 cups [840 g] chopped Vidalia onions

2 tsp sugar

1 cup [115 g] grated Gruyère cheese

2 Tbsp chopped fresh chives

1 cup [240 g] sour cream

1 cup [240 g] mayonnaise, best quality such as Hellmann's, Best Foods, or Duke's

3 oz [85 g] cream cheese, at room temperature

½ tsp Worcestershire sauce

½ tsp salt

¼ tsp freshly ground black pepper

Potato chips, baguette, or crackers, for serving

pro tips

Use a stainless-steel or cast-iron skillet when caramelizing onions; they won't brown as well in a nonstick pan.

To "deglaze" a pan is to add liquid such as stock, water, or wine to loosen and dissolve any flavorful food particles (sometimes called "fond") that are stuck to the bottom.

1. Preheat the oven to 425°F [220°C] and set an oven rack in the middle position.

2. In a large stainless-steel or cast-iron skillet, melt the butter over medium-high heat. Add the onions and 1 teaspoon of the sugar to the pan; sauté for 10 minutes, stirring frequently, until the onions are lightly browned.

3. Lower the heat to medium and cook, stirring frequently, until the onions are meltingly tender and a rich, deep caramel color, 20 to 25 minutes more. To help the caramelization process along and prevent the onions from burning, deglaze (see Pro Tip) the pan every so often with a few tablespoons of water—but wait to do this until you see a brown film forming on the bottom of the pan. I usually use about ¾ cup [180 ml] of water total, but you may need more or less.

4. Set aside 2 tablespoons of the Gruyère. In a medium bowl, combine the remaining Gruyère, remaining 1 teaspoon sugar, 1 tablespoon of the chives, the sour cream, mayonnaise, cream cheese, Worcestershire

sauce, salt, and pepper. Add the warm caramelized onions and mix until well combined.

5. Transfer the onion mixture to a 1½-qt [1.5-L] ovenproof serving dish. Sprinkle with the reserved Gruyère and bake for 15 to 20 minutes, until lightly browned and bubbly. Let the dip cool for about 10 minutes, then sprinkle with the remaining 1 tablespoon chives and serve with potato chips, a sliced baguette, or crackers. (If there is any grease on the top, blot it with a paper towel.)

MAKE AHEAD: This dip can be prepared several days ahead of time, refrigerated, and baked right before serving.

spanakopita rolls

TOP ON MY LIST at every Greek restaurant is spanakopita, the flaky phyllo pastry triangles stuffed with spinach and feta cheese, not least because they can be time-consuming to make at home. But this recipe proves they don't have to be. Instead of folding dozens of little triangles, I roll the spinach mixture into logs, which get sliced into rounds when they come out of the oven. The result: bite-sized spanakopita, in just an hour's time. Sometimes, I just cut the logs in half and serve them as a main course. With their buttery crust and rich spinach filling, they are definitely dinner worthy. Makes thirty 1-in [2.5-cm] rolls

2 Tbsp extra-virgin olive oil

½ cup [70 g] finely chopped yellow onion

Two 10-oz [280-g] boxes frozen chopped spinach, thawed and squeezed very dry

2 garlic cloves, minced

¾ tsp salt

½ tsp freshly ground black pepper

¼ cup [60 ml] heavy cream

1 Tbsp finely chopped fresh dill, or 1 tsp dried

⅛ tsp ground nutmeg

2 eggs, beaten

½ cup [55 g] crumbled feta cheese

¾ cup (1½ sticks) [165 g] unsalted butter, melted

½ lb [230 g] frozen phyllo dough, thawed in refrigerator overnight

sourcing savvy

Phyllo is a tissue-thin dough used for making flaky European and Middle Eastern pastries such as baklava, strudel, and spanakopita. You can find it in the freezer section of most grocery stores. Be sure to thaw it overnight in the refrigerator before using.

1. Preheat the oven to 375°F [190°C] and set an oven rack in the middle position. Line a rimmed 13-by-18-in [33-by-46-cm] baking sheet with parchment paper.

2. In a large skillet, warm the olive oil over medium heat. Add the onion and cook, stirring frequently, until softened, about 5 minutes. Add the spinach, garlic, salt, and pepper and cook, stirring frequently, for a few minutes more. Add the heavy cream, dill, and nutmeg and cook for 1 minute more, until the cream is fully absorbed into the spinach. Transfer the spinach mixture to a medium bowl. Let cool until warm to the touch.

3. Add the eggs and feta cheese to the spinach mixture and stir to combine. Set aside.

CONTINUED

pro tip

If you've never worked with phyllo, don't let it scare you off. It's very forgiving and just takes a little getting used to. Even if the dough falls apart in your hands, you can patch it right back together again. And as long as the top sheet of the phyllo looks good, I promise, no one will notice!

4. Wet and wring out a clean dish towel. Have the melted butter and a pastry brush nearby. Unroll the phyllo and cover it with the plastic wrap from the package (it's usually rolled in a sheet of plastic) or a sheet of wax paper, followed by the damp towel; be sure to keep it covered at all times so it doesn't dry out.

5. Remove one sheet of phyllo from the pile and gently spread it out horizontally on a clean, dry work surface so that a long edge is closest to you. Brush the dough evenly with melted butter. Place another sheet of phyllo on top of the first and brush it lightly with butter. Continue until you have five layers.

6. Spread one-third of the spinach mixture into a thick line over the phyllo along the long side near you, leaving a 2-in [5-cm] border at the bottom and a 1-in [2.5-cm] border along the short sides. Fold the sides of the phyllo over the spinach mixture; then roll fairly tightly into a log starting at the spinach end.

7. Transfer the assembled roll to the prepared baking sheet, seam-side down. Brush the top with butter. Repeat the process and make two more rolls with the remaining filling and dough. Using a sharp knife, score the top of the rolls at 1-in [2.5-cm] intervals, cutting through the top layers of phyllo dough just to the filling.

8. Bake for 30 to 35 minutes, until golden brown. Let stand for 10 minutes, and then transfer the logs to a cutting board. Cut into pieces and serve on a platter. (When cutting, use a chef's knife to make one quick downward motion on the score lines; do not using a "sawing" motion or the phyllo will be more apt to crumble.)

MAKE AHEAD: You can prepare the rolls and refrigerate them for up to 2 hours before baking. You can also wrap the individual rolls in heavy-duty aluminum foil and freeze for a few months. They can be baked directly from the freezer; just keep in mind that frozen rolls will take a bit longer to cook. (Leftovers reheat well in a 300°F [150°C] oven or toaster oven.)

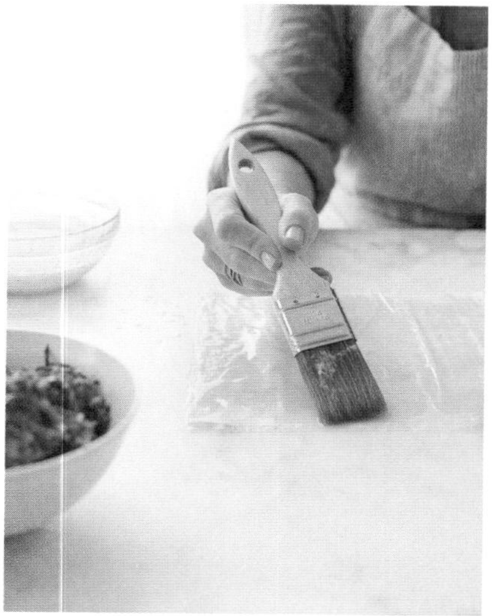
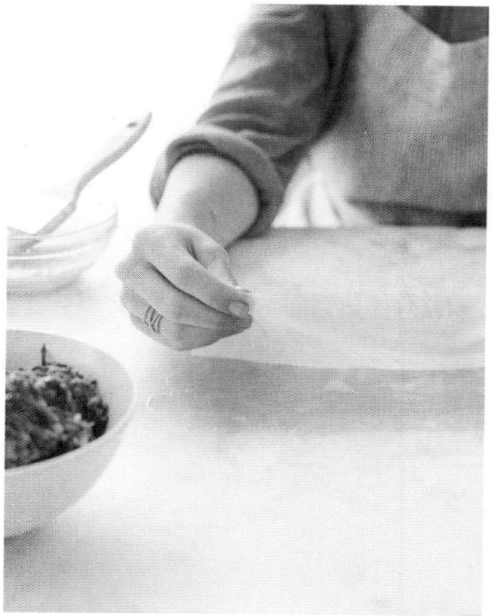
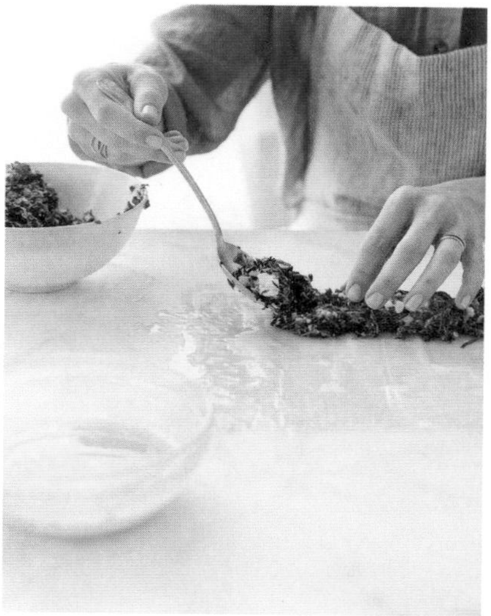
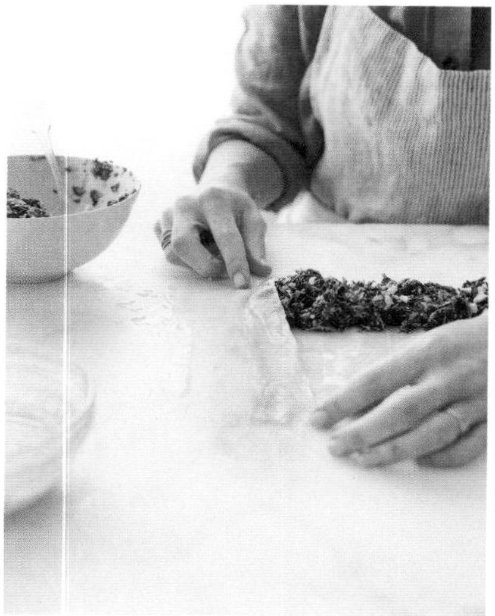
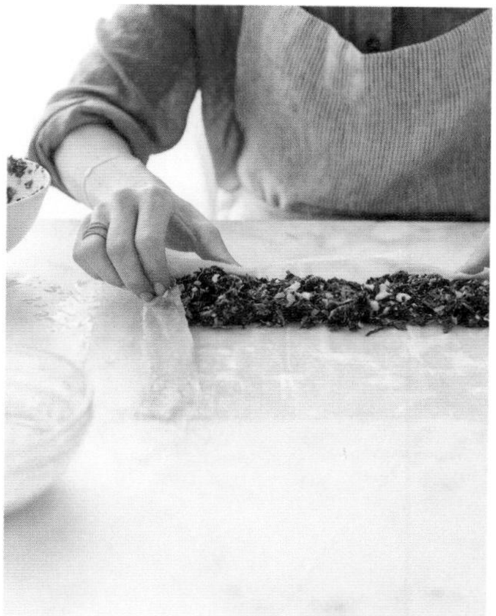
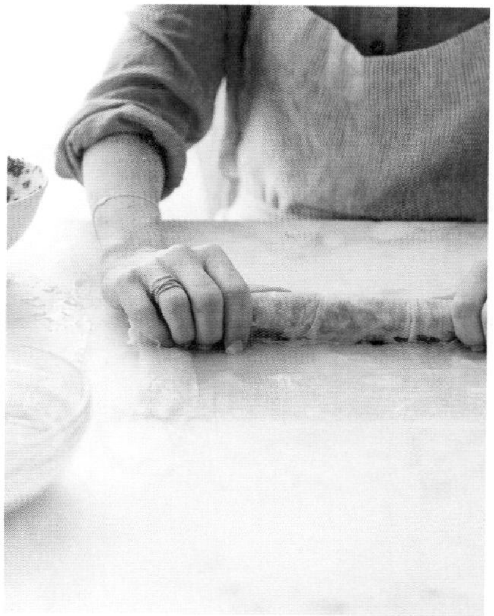
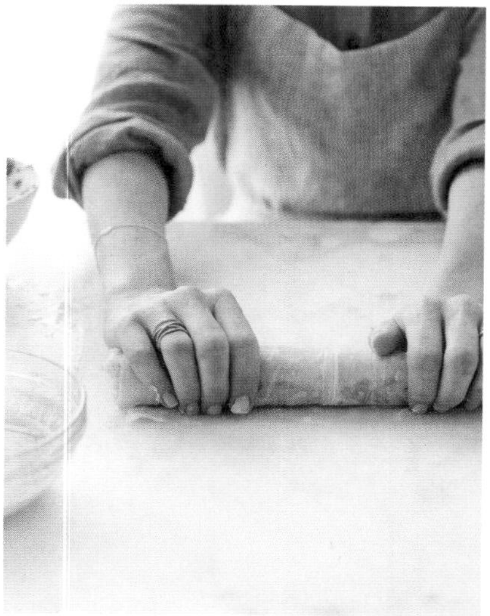
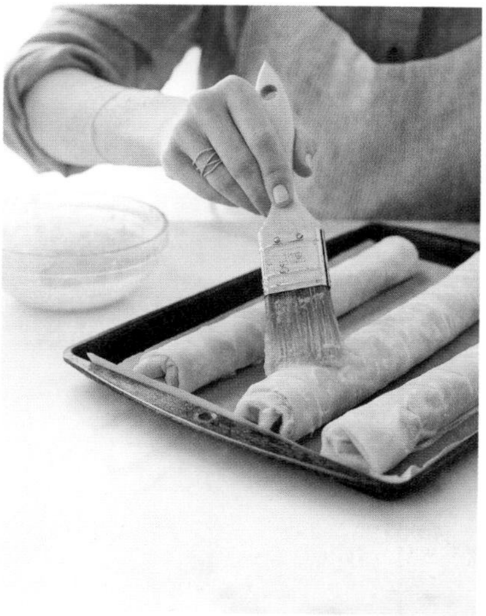
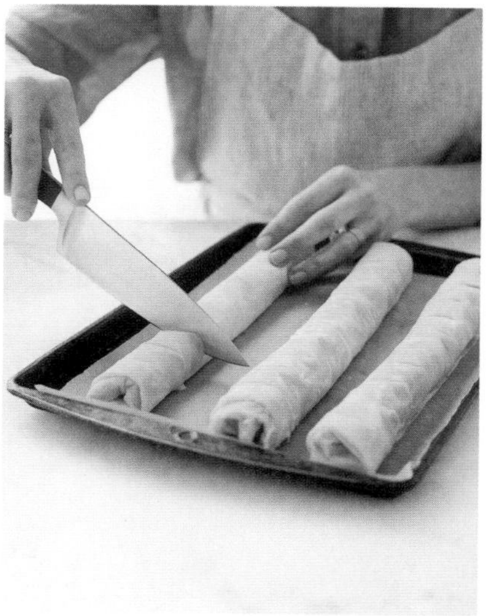

deviled eggs with candied bacon & chives

A LITTLE SWEET and crunchy bacon is a great way to jazz up classic deviled eggs. The only problem is that once you taste the candied bacon, you'll be tempted to forget the eggs entirely and eat the bacon on its own. No worries—I've called for a little extra in the recipe so you won't have to resist the temptation to sneak a few bites. Makes 12

sourcing savvy

If you want to save some time, feel free to buy already hard-boiled eggs, which are available at many grocery stores.

pro tip

For the creamiest, fluffiest, lump-free deviled egg filling, pass the yolks through a mesh sieve. (You can also blend the yolks in a food processor with the other filling ingredients for a similar result.)

4 slices bacon, cut into ½-in [12-mm] pieces

1½ tsp apple cider vinegar

2 tsp packed dark brown sugar

6 eggs

2 Tbsp mayonnaise, best quality such as Hellmann's, Best Foods, or Duke's

1 tsp Dijon mustard

¼ tsp Worcestershire sauce

⅛ tsp salt

⅛ tsp freshly ground black pepper

Pinch of cayenne pepper

2 tsp chopped fresh chives

1. Set a small nonstick skillet over medium heat. Add the bacon to the pan and cook, stirring frequently, until crisp and well rendered, 5 to 7 minutes. Using a slotted spoon, remove the bacon from the skillet. Pour the fat into a bowl—you'll use some of it later—and place the pan back on the stove (no need to clean it). Turn the heat to low and add 1 teaspoon of the vinegar and the brown sugar. Stir to dissolve the sugar, then add the bacon back to the pan. Cook, stirring constantly, until the bacon is evenly coated with the sugar mixture, about 1 minute. Transfer the bacon bits to a plate in a single layer (they'll stick together a bit; that's okay); let cool completely.

2. Place the eggs in a medium saucepan and fill the pan with enough water so that it covers the eggs by about 1 in [2.5 cm]. Bring to a boil over high heat, then remove the pan from the heat, cover, and let stand for 10 minutes. Place the hard-boiled eggs in a bowl of cold water to cool (I usually just use the saucepan).

3. Crack the eggs, then peel under cold running water. Slice the eggs in half lengthwise. Remove the yolks and place them in a small bowl. Arrange the whites on a serving platter. Using a spatula, push the yolks through a mesh sieve into a bowl (see Pro Tip). Add 1 tablespoon of the reserved bacon fat, the remaining ½ teaspoon vinegar, the mayonnaise, mustard, Worcestershire sauce, salt, pepper, and cayenne. Use a small

rubber spatula to mix, smearing the mixture against the side of the bowl, until smooth. Taste and adjust the seasoning, if necessary.

4. Fill a sealable plastic bag with the yolk mixture, and use your fingers to push the mixture to one corner of the bag. Use scissors to snip off the tip of the corner, opening up a ¼-in [6-mm] hole. Pipe the yolk mixture evenly into the egg-white halves. (Alternatively, for a less fussy preparation, simply spoon the yolk mixture into the egg whites.) Top with the cooled candied bacon, sprinkle with the chives, and serve.

MAKE AHEAD: The eggs can be cooked and stored whole in the refrigerator several days ahead of time, and the bacon can be made a few hours ahead. Assemble the deviled eggs at the last minute so that the bacon stays crisp.

ahi tuna poke with avocado & rice crackers

TUNA POKE (pronounced *po-kay*) is a traditional Hawaiian salad of raw tuna marinated in soy sauce, sesame oil, and onions. Here, I've prepared it as a tartare by finely dicing the tuna and serving it with crispy rice crackers. Tartare is usually thought of as a fancy restaurant dish, but now that sushi-grade tuna is readily available at many markets, it's really easy to make at home. Serves 4 to 6

sourcing savvy

When selecting tuna for tartare, be sure to get fresh, sushi-grade yellowfin or big-eye tuna (both referred to as "ahi"), with a pink or reddish color. Whole Foods carries a great frozen product called "Sushi at Home" that is sold in convenient ½-lb [230-g] packages. Avoid albacore tuna, which is the white tuna used to make canned tuna fish.

3 Tbsp soy sauce (not low-sodium)

1 Tbsp Asian sesame oil

1 Tbsp vegetable oil, plus more for greasing

1 Tbsp drained and minced pickled ginger from a jar (peeled and minced fresh ginger may be substituted)

1 Tbsp fresh lime juice, from 1 lime

1 Tbsp seeded and minced jalapeño pepper, from 1 pepper

1½ tsp sugar

¼ tsp crushed red pepper flakes (optional)

2 scallions, white and green parts, thinly sliced

½ lb [230 g] sushi-grade tuna such as ahi, cut into ¼-in [6-mm] dice

1 large avocado, pitted, peeled, and diced

1 tsp black or white sesame seeds, for garnish (optional)

Rice crackers, for serving

1. In a medium bowl, whisk together the soy sauce, sesame oil, vegetable oil, ginger, lime juice, jalapeño, sugar, red pepper flakes (if using), and scallions. Set aside.

2. Right before serving, add the diced tuna to the sauce and stir to combine. Fold in the avocado with a rubber spatula, taking care not to smash the avocado.

3. Lightly grease a round 1-cup dry measuring cup or 3-in [7.5-cm] diameter ramekin to use as a mold. Pack half of the tuna and avocado mixture into the cup, then carefully flip it out onto a serving platter to form a tower. It should slide out easily, but you may need to tap it against the platter to nudge it out. Wipe out the cup, grease again, and repeat with the remaining mixture, forming a second tower (either on the same platter or a different platter). Sprinkle with sesame seeds, if desired. Serve immediately with small spoons for scooping the tartare onto rice crackers.

MAKE AHEAD: It's fine to prepare the sauce and dice the tuna a few hours ahead of time and store separately in covered containers in the refrigerator. But wait to cut the avocado and mix everything together until right before serving.

maryland-style crab cakes with quick tartar sauce

heads up

Allow 1 hour for the crab cakes to set in the refrigerator before cooking.

WHEN YOU LIVE IN MARYLAND, eating Chesapeake blue crabs is practically a religion—and in my family, we are all loyal devotees. Every summer, we hit all of our favorite crab shacks, from local joints all the way to the Eastern Shore, where you can look out over the bay and put your feet in the sand.

I'd never attempt making steamed crabs at home. Live crabs, giant steamers—yikes! But I do often make Maryland-style crab cakes, which are just as delicious and easier to prepare (not to mention eat). These are made with fresh lump crabmeat and just enough filler to bind the crabmeat together. I love them with the Quick Tartar Sauce below, but you can also serve them with lemon wedges or cocktail sauce.

Celery is not traditional in Maryland crab cakes, but I love the little crunch it adds. Feel free to leave it out if you're a purist. Makes 12 mini crab cakes

sourcing savvy

If you can only find jumbo lump crabmeat, you may need to break the pieces up a bit. If the clumps are too large, the crab cakes won't hold together well.

FOR THE CRAB CAKES

2 eggs

2½ Tbsp mayonnaise, best quality such as Hellmann's, Best Foods, or Duke's

1½ tsp Dijon mustard

1 tsp Worcestershire sauce

1 tsp Old Bay seasoning

¼ tsp salt

¼ cup [30 g] finely diced celery (optional)

2 Tbsp finely chopped fresh Italian parsley

1 lb [455 g] lump crabmeat

½ cup [30 g] panko

Vegetable or canola oil, for cooking

FOR THE QUICK TARTAR SAUCE

1 cup [240 g] mayonnaise, best quality such as Hellmann's, Best Foods, or Duke's

1½ Tbsp sweet pickle relish

1 tsp Dijon mustard

1 Tbsp minced red onion

1½ Tbsp fresh lemon juice, from 1 lemon

Salt and freshly ground black pepper, to taste

CONTINUED

1. Line a baking sheet with aluminum foil for easy cleanup.

2. To make the crab cakes: Combine the eggs, mayonnaise, mustard, Worcestershire, Old Bay, salt, celery (if using), and parsley in a large bowl and mix well. Add the crabmeat (be sure to check it for any cartilage) and panko; gently fold the mixture together until just combined, being careful not to shred the crabmeat. Shape into 12 mini crab cakes, about ¼ cup [50 g] each, and place on the prepared baking sheet. Cover and refrigerate for at least 1 hour.

3. Meanwhile, make the tartar sauce: Mix all the ingredients together in a small bowl. Taste and adjust the seasoning, if necessary. Cover and chill until ready to serve.

4. Preheat a large nonstick pan over medium heat and coat with oil. When the oil is hot, place the crab cakes in the pan and cook until golden brown, about 3 to 5 minutes per side. Be careful, as the oil may splatter.

5. Serve the crab cakes warm with the tartar sauce.

MAKE AHEAD: The crab cakes can be formed, covered, and refrigerated a day ahead of time before cooking. The tartar sauce can be made and refrigerated up to 2 days in advance.

grilled beef satay
with peanut sauce

THIS IS ONE OF MY FAVORITE RECIPES in this book. And even though it's in the appetizer chapter, I often serve it for dinner. The whole family loves it, and the payoff in flavor is totally disproportionate to the effort involved. The hardest part—and, believe me, it's not hard—is slicing the beef. After that, you simply whirl the marinade in a blender, slather it on the beef, and grill. The sauce comes together in a flash, too.

There's no need to wait for grilling weather to make these. I've cooked them under the broiler and in a stovetop grill pan (many times without the skewers, if I'm feeling lazy), always with success. Metal or wooden skewers may be used. You'll need about 24 short skewers or 12 long ones. Serves 6 to 8 as an appetizer; 3 to 4 as a main course

heads up

When you read through the recipe, you might wonder if I forgot the step of marinating the beef. I assure you, I didn't! The marinade is thick and clings to the meat, imparting loads of flavor in the short time it takes to cook. Go ahead and marinate longer if you want to get a head start, but know that it doesn't make a bit of difference in terms of flavor.

FOR THE PEANUT SAUCE

¾ cup [180 ml] unsweetened coconut milk

¼ cup [65 g] creamy peanut butter

3 Tbsp packed dark brown sugar

1 Tbsp Thai red curry paste

1 Tbsp Sriracha

1 Tbsp fish sauce

2 Tbsp fresh lime juice, from 1 lime (use the lime you zest for the marinade)

FOR THE BEEF

One 1½-lb [680-g] flank steak

6 Tbsp [90 ml] vegetable oil

1½ Tbsp fish sauce

1½ Tbsp soy sauce

3 Tbsp packed dark brown sugar

2 garlic cloves, roughly chopped

Zest from 1 lime

¾ tsp crushed red pepper flakes

1 tsp ground coriander

1 tsp ground cumin

1 tsp ground ginger

sourcing savvy

Flank steak is a tough cut but it works beautifully in this recipe because of the short cooking time. To guarantee that the meat is tender, be sure to cut it against (that is, perpendicular to) the grain. This cuts through the fibers and shortens them, making the meat easier to chew, since breaking up the muscle fibers has already been done for you. If you can't find flank steak, skirt steak is a good substitute.

Thai red curry paste, Sriracha, and fish sauce can all be found in the Asian food section of most large supermarkets.

CONTINUED

1. To make the peanut sauce: In a small saucepan, whisk all of the ingredients together over high heat. Bring to a boil, then lower the heat and simmer until slightly thickened, about 3 minutes. Set aside; the sauce will continue to thicken as it cools.

2. To make the beef satay: Cut the flank steak against the grain into slices, about ¼ in [6 mm] thick. Place the steak slices in a medium bowl and set aside.

3. Combine the remaining ingredients in a blender and purée until smooth and thick. Pour the mixture over the steak slices and toss until evenly coated.

4. Thread the sliced meat onto 24 short or 12 long skewers and lay flat on an aluminum foil–lined baking sheet. Pour any marinade that's left in the bowl over the beef skewers.

5. Preheat the grill to high, then oil the grates. Grill the skewers, covered, until the beef is browned on the outside but still pink on the inside, 1 to 2 minutes per side. Serve the satay warm with the peanut sauce on the side.

pro tips

If using wooden skewers, be sure to soak them in water for 20 to 30 minutes prior to using.

To make the steak a cinch to cut, stick it in the freezer for 10 to 15 minutes before slicing.

mastering salt

I will admit, at the risk of being barred from dinner parties in the future, that whenever I have a meal at someone's house, I position the salt shaker near my plate so that I can covertly salt my food during the meal without insulting my host. The fact is, most people are so afraid of over-salting their food that they drastically under-salt it. Unfortunately, this makes even the most lovingly prepared food taste bland. And you can't completely salvage a bland dish once it's cooked. Food tastes best when it is seasoned gradually during the cooking process.

Mastering salt is one of the first lessons I learned in culinary school. During the first week of class, my chef instructor lined up ten bowls of chicken broth on a table: the first bowl had no salt and the last bowl had the most salt. Every student was given ten spoons and asked to taste each bowl of broth and pick the one that was seasoned properly. The first few bowls were bland like dishwater, as expected, but as I tasted each bowl along the way, I kept thinking: *This is it! This one has the perfect amount of salt.* But as I continued to move down the line, each bowl tasted better than the last. When I got to the final bowl, which I initially assumed must be way over-salted, I tasted it and found the perfectly seasoned bowl of broth. It made all the others before it taste bland. This was an *aha!* moment for me. I realized that chefs push salt to the absolute limit, which is why their food is so flavorful.

DIFFERENT TYPES OF SALT TO KEEP IN YOUR KITCHEN AND WHEN TO USE THEM

It's fun to play with different types of salt (I love pink salt and smoked sea salt), but you really only need to keep three types of salt in your kitchen: table salt or fine sea salt (they're almost identical), kosher salt, and flaky sea salt. They all taste pretty much the same, but they're not interchangeable in recipes unless you measure by weight. Table salt is finer than kosher salt and flaky sea salt, so a teaspoon of table salt is more salt than a teaspoon of kosher or flaky sea salt.

fine sea salt & table salt

For the recipes in this book, unless they specify otherwise, I use ordinary table salt or fine sea salt. The difference between them is that table salt is mined from underground salt deposits, while fine sea salt is made directly through the evaporation of seawater. Sea salt is marketed as healthier and fancier but, truthfully, it tastes almost identical to table salt and has the same basic nutritional value.

kosher salt

Because it has large crystals, which are easier to feel, sprinkle, and see, chefs often use kosher salt for seasoning meat and fish before cooking. Contrary to popular belief, it does not taste any better or different than table salt.

flaky sea salt

Flaky sea salt is expensive, so it shouldn't be used for cooking, but rather for adding a crunchy, salty finishing touch to a dish. It's wonderful on both savory and sweet foods. Try a few crunchy flakes sprinkled on a steak, a buttered baguette, or chocolate.

soups & sandwiches

Growing up with two grandmothers who considered chicken soup to be the world's best medicine ("Jewish penicillin," as it's sometimes called), I was raised on the notion that soup can cure all manner of ills. Whenever my little sister or I got sick, my Nonny would tell my mother to ignore the advice of the doctor, throw away the medicine, and make a pot of chicken matzo ball soup.

I'm not as old-school as my grandmothers—believe me, I'm the first one to pop an aspirin—but there's no denying that when you're feeling down, stressed out, or under the weather, a bowl of soup can make you feel better. I even find *making* soup to be therapeutic. Not only is it forgiving—you barely need to measure—soup is well suited to big-batch cooking and freezing. While I've never been one to freeze meals (anything I optimistically freeze inevitably gets forgotten and thrown away), soup is the exception; and it makes me happy to know that my efforts will result in convenient sustenance at some point down the road. For instance, when I come drooping in the door at night and can't muster the energy to cook, it's a relief to know that I can plunk an icy block of soup in a pot and have dinner ready in the time it takes to change into my cozy clothes.

All that said, don't think these recipes are just for comfort on dreary winter days. When it's a sticky inferno outside, a bowl of golden gazpacho is gloriously refreshing. And, of course, you can't have soup without sandwiches; I think you'll love the fun twists on grilled cheese (page 78) and avocado toast (page 74) at the chapter's end.

golden orange gazpacho with basil

FRESH-SQUEEZED ORANGE JUICE highlights the flavor of golden cherry tomatoes and makes this soup taste like pure sunshine. It's the sort of thing you can keep in the fridge in the summertime, eat three times a week, and never tire of. And it's good for you, too. Serves 6

heads up

Allow at least 2 hours for this soup to chill in the fridge.

¾ cup [105 g] roughly chopped red onion

2 lb [910 g] golden cherry tomatoes

1 yellow bell pepper, seeded and roughly chopped

1 English (hothouse) cucumber, seeded and diced (do not peel)

⅓ cup [15 g] packed fresh basil leaves, roughly chopped

⅓ cup [80 ml] extra-virgin olive oil

2 tsp salt

¼ tsp freshly ground black pepper

1 tsp sugar

2 Tbsp white wine vinegar

Juice of 3 large oranges (about 1½ cups [360 ml])

½ cup [120 ml] water

½ to ¾ tsp hot-pepper sauce, to taste

pro tip

Because their skin is very thin and unwaxed, English cucumbers do not need to be peeled. The flecks of green skin look pretty in this soup.

1. Place the onions in a small bowl and cover with water. Let soak for 10 minutes, then drain.

2. In a food processor fitted with the steel blade, combine half of the tomatoes, half of the bell pepper, half of the cucumber, and half of the drained onion. Pulse until finely chopped but not puréed, 25 to 30 one-second pulses. Transfer the mixture to a large bowl. Add the remaining tomatoes, bell pepper, cucumber, and onion, along with all of the basil, to the food processor (no need to wipe the bowl clean beforehand). Process until the vegetables are finely chopped, 25 to 30 one-second pulses, then add to the bowl with the other vegetables.

3. Add the remaining ingredients to the vegetable mixture and stir to combine. Chill until cold, at least 2 hours. Before serving, taste and adjust the seasoning, if necessary. Ladle into bowls and serve cold. This soup is best served fresh, but will keep in the refrigerator for up to 2 days.

chilled cucumber & yogurt soup

heads up

This soup will seem a little thin straight out of the blender, but it thickens up nicely as it chills. Plan to make it at least 2 hours ahead of time if possible.

THE CLASSIC COMBINATION of cucumber and yogurt is refreshing and spa-like, so you can't help but feel virtuous sipping on this soup. The best part is that it can be whirled up in a blender in just 15 minutes without ever turning on the stove. Moreover, it's a great way to use up the bounty of cucumbers in the summer. Serves 4

3 English (hothouse) cucumbers

1½ cups [360 g] plain Greek yogurt (whole milk or 2 percent; do not use nonfat)

3 Tbsp extra-virgin olive oil

1 tsp white wine vinegar

1½ tsp salt

¼ tsp freshly ground black pepper

½ cup [20 g] packed fresh mint leaves

2 Tbsp chopped fresh dill, plus a few more small sprigs for serving

1 small garlic clove

Pinch of sugar

3 Tbsp chopped fresh chives, for serving

Store-bought pita chips, crushed, for serving

pro tip

While English cucumbers don't need to be peeled, the texture of this soup is better without the skin.

1. Cut a 2-in [5-cm] chunk off the end of one of the cucumbers and set aside (later, you'll cut it into rounds for garnishing the soup). Peel the remaining cucumbers with a vegetable peeler. Cut the peeled cucumbers in half lengthwise, then use a small spoon to scrape out the seeds. Chop the seeded cucumbers into ½-in [12-mm] chunks.

2. In a blender, combine the cucumbers along with all of the other ingredients except for the chives and pita chips. Purée until completely smooth. Pour the soup into a bowl or pitcher, cover with plastic wrap, and refrigerate until chilled and thickened, at least 2 hours. This soup will keep nicely in the refrigerator for up to 3 days.

3. Right before serving, slice the reserved cucumber into very thin rounds (they should be light enough to float). Ladle or pour the soup into serving bowls and garnish with the chives, cucumber slices, dill sprigs, and crushed pita chips.

fiery roasted-tomato basil soup

serve with smoked gouda & pesto grilled cheese sandwiches
(PAGE 78).

heads up

I call this soup "fiery" because of the warmth of flavor that comes from roasting the vegetables, but also because it's got some kick. The recipe calls for only ¼ teaspoon of red pepper flakes, but it's spicier than you'd expect. If you're heat-sensitive, add the pepper flakes to taste.

WHEN MY KIDS WERE TODDLERS, I had a full-blown vegetable garden in the backyard. While I weeded and harvested, the kids would fill up their little watering cans at the outdoor faucet and then waddle back and forth to the garden, spilling most of the water en route and sprinkling just a tiny bit on the plants each time. It kept them busy for hours! I originally came up with this recipe as a way to use up all of my home-grown tomatoes, but I still make it whether I have my own tomato plants or not. Roasting the vegetables intensifies their flavor, brings out their sweetness, and adds a subtle hint of smokiness. Serves 4 to 6

2½ lb [1.1 kg] plum tomatoes, halved

2 small yellow onions, quartered

6 garlic cloves

¼ cup [60 ml] extra-virgin olive oil

1½ tsp salt

Freshly ground black pepper

4 cups [1 L] low-sodium chicken broth

1 Tbsp sugar

2 bay leaves

¼ tsp crushed red pepper flakes

⅓ cup [15 g] packed fresh basil leaves, roughly chopped, plus more for garnish

⅓ cup [80 ml] heavy cream

pro tip

Line your baking sheet with heavy-duty aluminum foil. When done, simply lift the foil and slide all of the roasted vegetables—with their juices—right into the pot.

1. Preheat the oven to 450°F [230°C] and set an oven rack in the middle position. Line a rimmed 13-by-18-in [33-by-46-cm] baking sheet with heavy-duty aluminum foil for easy cleanup.

2. Arrange the tomatoes and onions, cut-sides up, on the prepared baking sheet. Scatter the garlic around the pan. Drizzle the vegetables with the oil and sprinkle with 1 teaspoon of the salt and ½ teaspoon black pepper. Roast for 30 to 35 minutes, until the onions are browned on top and the tomatoes are golden and caramelized on the bottom.

3. Remove the vegetables from the oven and transfer to a large (6-qt [6-L]) soup pot; be sure to add the juices from the pan, too. Add the remaining ½ teaspoon salt, the chicken broth, sugar, bay leaves, and red pepper flakes; bring to a boil. Lower the heat and simmer, uncovered, for 20 minutes.

4. Remove and discard the bay leaves. Off the heat, use a handheld immersion blender to purée the soup until completely smooth.

(Alternatively, let the soup cool slightly and use a blender to purée in batches. Be sure to remove the center knob on the blender top and cover with a dish towel to avoid splatters.) Add the basil and blend until finely chopped. Stir in the cream and bring to a simmer over medium heat. Taste and adjust the seasoning, if necessary. Ladle the soup into bowls and garnish with more chopped basil. Serve hot.

MAKE AHEAD: This soup will keep nicely in the fridge for 3 to 4 days. It can also be frozen for up to 3 months, but hold off on adding the cream until reheating.

autumn curried carrot & sweet potato soup

IT SEEMS I'VE ALWAYS got the components of this soup lingering in my veggie bin (along with other mysterious things, but I'll spare you those details), so it's easy to whip up on a cool fall day. The nice thing is that the sweet potatoes add body to the soup, making it luxuriously silky, without even the slightest bit of guilt-inducing heavy cream. Now, I have to admit that I'm not one of those people who look forward to fall: my pessimistic side knows all too well that winter is looming. But the thought of comfort food and cozy clothes does make it more bearable. So go ahead and think of this soup as that soft sweater you can't wait to put on at the first sign of a chill. Serves 8

4 Tbsp [55 g] unsalted butter

2 cups [280 g] chopped yellow onions

1 Tbsp curry powder, plus a bit more for serving (optional)

1 lb [455 g] carrots, peeled and chopped into 1-in [2.5-cm] pieces

1½ lb [680 g] sweet potatoes (about 2 small), peeled and chopped into 1-in [2.5-cm] pieces

8 cups [2 L] low-sodium chicken broth

1¾ tsp salt

1 tart yet sweet apple (such as Honeycrisp or Fuji), peeled, cored, and chopped

2 Tbsp honey

Freshly ground black pepper

sourcing savvy

It's common practice in the United States to use the words "sweet potato" and "yam" interchangeably. This is confusing since yams aren't sweet potatoes at all, but rather, thick white tubers with dark brown skins. Chances are you won't find real yams at the supermarket, so if you see "yams," you're probably looking at sweet potatoes.

1. In a large pot, melt the butter over medium heat. Add the onions and cook, stirring frequently, until soft and translucent, about 10 minutes. Do not brown. Add the curry powder and cook a minute more.

2. Add the carrots, sweet potatoes, chicken broth, and salt and bring to a boil. Cover and simmer over low heat until the vegetables are very tender, about 25 minutes. Stir in the apple and honey. Using a handheld immersion blender, purée the soup until smooth and creamy. (Alternatively, let the soup cool slightly and use a blender to purée in batches. Be sure to remove the center knob on the blender top and cover with a dish towel to avoid splatters.) Season to taste with salt, pepper, and more honey, if necessary. Ladle the soup into bowls and sprinkle with more curry powder, if desired.

pro tip

Soups often thicken after they've sat for a while. The trick is to add a bit of water or broth while reheating—this will help to thin the soup back out.

MAKE AHEAD: This soup will keep nicely in the refrigerator for up to 4 days. It can also be frozen for up to 3 months.

creamy wild mushroom soup with herbs

AROUND HOLIDAY TIME, most grocers sell wild mushrooms in packages that are washed, sliced, and ready to cook, making this soup easy to throw together. What makes it unique is that some of the wine is added at the end—meaning it's not cooked off—which adds bright flavor that cuts through the earthiness of the mushrooms and richness of the cream. I love this soup as a starter for a dinner party—it's creamy and flavorful, yet not so rich that it spoils everyone's appetite. Serves 4 to 6

4 Tbsp [55 g] unsalted butter

1 cup [150 g] chopped shallots

4 garlic cloves, roughly chopped

¼ cup [30 g] all-purpose flour

1½ lb [680 g] mixed wild mushrooms (such as shiitake, oyster, portobello), stemmed and roughly chopped

½ cup [120 ml] dry white wine

5 cups [1.2 L] low-sodium chicken broth

1¼ tsp salt

½ tsp freshly ground black pepper

½ cup [120 ml] heavy cream

1 tsp finely chopped fresh thyme

1 tsp finely chopped fresh sage

1 Tbsp finely chopped fresh chives, for garnish

Homemade Herb Croutons (recipe follows) or store-bought croutons for garnish

pro tip

It's fine to buy prepared produce from the supermarket but remember the grocer's rule: first in, first out. The oldest packages will be in the front. For the freshest produce, reach to the back of the shelf and you'll typically find packages with a later expiration date.

1. In a large pot, melt the butter over medium-low heat. Add the shallots and cook, stirring occasionally, until softened, about 4 minutes. Add the garlic and cook 2 minutes more. Stir in the flour and cook 1 minute more, then add the mushrooms, ¼ cup [60 ml] of the wine, the chicken broth, salt, and pepper. Bring to a boil, then lower the heat and simmer, uncovered, for 15 minutes, until the mushrooms are tender.

2. Using a slotted spoon, remove about 2 large ladlefuls of the mushrooms and set aside (don't worry if there are some shallots mixed in there). Using a handheld immersion blender, purée the soup until smooth. (Alternatively, let the soup cool slightly and use a blender to purée in batches. Be sure to remove the center knob on the blender top and cover with a dish towel to avoid splatters.)

CONTINUED

3. Stir in the cream, the remaining ¼ cup [60 ml] wine, the thyme, the sage, and the reserved mushrooms. Bring to a simmer, then taste and adjust the seasoning with salt and pepper, if necessary. Ladle into bowls and top with the chives and croutons.

MAKE AHEAD: This soup will keep nicely in the refrigerator for 3 to 4 days.

homemade herb croutons

STORE-BOUGHT CROUTONS are fine in a pinch—although look for freshly made rather than boxed—but there's nothing like home-made. Plus, it's a tasty way to use up any stale bread you've got lying around.

2 cups [100 g] cubed French or Italian bread, preferably day old

2 Tbsp unsalted butter, melted

2 tsp finely chopped mixed fresh herbs, such as parsley, thyme, chives, sage, and/or rosemary

Salt and freshly ground black pepper

1. Preheat the oven to 375°F [190°C] and set an oven rack in the middle position. Line a 13-by-18-in [33-by-46-cm] baking sheet with heavy-duty aluminum foil for easy cleanup.

2. Directly on the prepared baking sheet, toss the bread cubes with the melted butter and herbs. Sprinkle with a pinch of salt and a few grinds of black pepper. Bake for 13 to 15 minutes, tossing once, until the bread cubes are golden brown and crisp. Let cool and store in an airtight container at room temperature for up to 3 days, or in the freezer for several weeks.

chicken tortilla soup

WHENEVER WE VISIT MY PARENTS in Longboat Key, Florida, we spend a lot of time hanging out at St. Armands Circle. It's the kind of place where you stroll in and out of boutiques, people-watch at sidewalk cafés, walk around with drippy ice cream cones, and ask every stranger with a dog if your children can pet it. One of our favorite restaurants there is Tommy Bahama. The food's always good, and we love sitting at a big round table under gently spinning wicker fans, listening to a one-man band play endless Jimmy Buffet tunes. We all have our favorite dishes at Tommy's, but one thing everyone agrees on is the chicken tortilla soup, made from puréed vegetables and tortillas. This is my version—lightened up a bit from the original but just as satisfying. Serves 6

¼ cup [60 ml] extra-virgin olive oil

4 Tbsp [55 g] unsalted butter

2½ cups [350 g] roughly chopped yellow onions

4 garlic cloves, cut into quarters

1 green bell pepper, seeded and roughly chopped

6 small (6-in [15-cm]) corn tortillas, cut into small pieces

1 Tbsp ground cumin

2 tsp chili powder

8 cups [2 L] low-sodium chicken broth

1½ tsp salt

¼ tsp cayenne pepper

OPTIONAL ADDITIONS

2 cooked skinless chicken breasts, cut into bite-sized pieces

Crushed tortilla chips

Fresh chopped cilantro

1 to 2 avocados, peeled, pitted, and diced

sourcing savvy

I usually use leftover or rotisserie chicken for this soup, but if you want to cook the chicken from scratch, you'll need two bone-in chicken breasts. Preheat the oven to 425°F [220°C] and set an oven rack in the middle position. Place the chicken breasts on an aluminum foil–lined baking sheet, season with salt and pepper, and cook for 35 to 40 minutes, or until the chicken is cooked through. Let cool, then pull the meat off the bone and cut into bite-sized pieces.

1. In a large pot, heat the oil and butter over medium heat. Add the onions, garlic, and green pepper and cook, stirring occasionally, until tender and just starting to brown, about 15 minutes. (Turn the heat to medium-low if the mixture is browning too quickly.)

2. Add the cut tortillas, cumin, and chili powder; continue to cook, stirring occasionally, a few minutes more. Add the chicken broth, salt, and cayenne and bring to a boil. Turn the heat down to low and simmer, uncovered, for about 20 minutes.

CONTINUED

3. Remove the pot from the heat, then use a handheld immersion blender to purée the soup until completely smooth. (Alternatively, let the soup cool slightly and use a blender to purée in batches. Be sure to remove the center knob on the blender top and cover with a dish towel to avoid splatters.) Stir in the chicken, if using, then ladle the soup into bowls and garnish with the tortilla chips, cilantro, and avocados, as you like.

MAKE AHEAD: This soup will keep nicely in the fridge for 3 to 4 days, and can be frozen for up to 3 months. However, it will thicken up quite a bit, so add a bit of water or chicken broth while reheating to thin it out as necessary.

pasta e fagioli

serve with celery, toasted walnut & pecorino salad (PAGE 95)
and garlic & herb ciabatta (PAGE 237).

PASTA E FAGIOLI, LITERALLY "pasta and beans," is a heartwarming Italian soup, perfect for a chilly night. This version—adapted from a recipe by Joe Cicala, executive chef at Le Virtù in Philadelphia, and featured in *The Washington Post*—is the best I've tried. The broth is thickened slightly with puréed beans, which makes it rich and satisfying. Serves 4

sourcing savvy

Pancetta is Italian cured pork belly, often referred to as "Italian bacon." However, it is not smoked like American bacon. You can often find pancetta conveniently diced and prepackaged in containers near the deli section. Otherwise, it is sold at the deli counter.

2 Tbsp extra-virgin olive oil, plus more for serving

4 oz [115 g] pancetta, diced

1 cup [140 g] finely chopped yellow onions

2 medium carrots, peeled and finely diced

2 medium celery stalks, finely diced

2 garlic cloves, minced

½ cup [120 ml] dry white wine

6 cups [1.4 L] low-sodium chicken broth

1 tsp salt

¼ tsp freshly ground black pepper

Two 15½-oz [445-g] cans cannellini beans or chickpeas (or a combination), drained and rinsed

¼ cup [50 g] dried French green lentils, rinsed (any green or brown lentils may be substituted)

1 cup [230 g] diced or chopped canned tomatoes, with their juices

2 bay leaves

1 Tbsp minced fresh rosemary

¾ cup [105 g] dried small pasta, such as elbow macaroni or ditalini

⅓ cup [35 g] freshly grated Parmigiano-Reggiano cheese, plus more for serving

1. In a large pot, heat the oil over medium-low heat. Add the pancetta and cook until the fat begins to render, about 5 minutes. Add the onions, carrots, and celery and increase the heat to medium. Cook, stirring frequently, until the onions become translucent, about 5 minutes. Add the garlic and cook for 1 minute more, stirring constantly so the garlic doesn't stick to the bottom of the pan and burn.

CONTINUED

2. Add the wine and cook until it has nearly evaporated, about 5 minutes. Add the broth, salt, pepper, beans, lentils, tomatoes, bay leaves, and rosemary. Increase the heat to high and bring to a boil, then decrease the heat to medium-low and simmer, uncovered, until the lentils are just tender, 15 to 30 minutes, depending on the type of lentils.

3. Use a slotted spoon to transfer 1 cup [240 ml] of the bean mixture and a little liquid to a blender. Remove the center knob of the blender top so the steam can escape. Hold a paper towel or kitchen towel over the opening to prevent splatters. Purée until smooth and set aside.

4. Add the pasta to the pot and stir to incorporate. Turn the heat up to a gentle boil and cook until the pasta is tender but still firm to the bite, anywhere from 8 to 12 minutes, depending on the type of pasta. The soup will thicken a bit by the time the pasta is cooked. Remove and discard the bay leaves.

5. Stir the reserved puréed bean mixture into the soup. (If you're having a hard time getting the mixture out of the blender, remove as much as you can with a rubber spatula, then add some of the hot soup broth to it and swirl around to loosen it up; it should come right out.) Cook briefly until the soup is heated through.

6. Remove the soup from the heat and stir in the Parmigiano-Reggiano. If the soup seems too thick, gradually add 1 to 2 cups [240 to 480 ml] of water or chicken broth to thin to the desired consistency. Season to taste with salt and pepper. Ladle the soup into bowls, drizzle each portion with a touch of olive oil, and sprinkle with more cheese, if desired. This soup is best served immediately; as it sits, the pasta and beans soak up the broth. If the soup gets too thick, thin it with a bit of broth or water.

hearty beef, barley & vegetable stoup

I BELIEVE IT WAS RACHAEL RAY who coined the word "stoup," and this rich broth teeming with chewy barley and vegetables is a perfect example of what stoup is: thicker than soup but thinner than stew. On a winter day, it will warm your bones from the inside out. Moreover, it makes a ton and freezes well, so you can check off two meals at once. This soup has saved me on many a snow day, when I've been stuck in the house with no food, no plow, and starving snow-drenched kids to feed. Just a quick defrost—then feed 'em, dress 'em, and they're out the door again. Serves 6

1½ lb [680 g] well-marbled beef chuck, trimmed of excess fat and cut into 1-in [2.5-cm] cubes

½ tsp freshly ground black pepper

1½ tsp salt

2 Tbsp vegetable oil

1¼ cups [175 g] chopped yellow onions

1 large celery stalk, thinly sliced

3 garlic cloves, roughly chopped

1½ Tbsp tomato paste

¾ cup [180 ml] red wine (any dry red will work, such as Pinot Noir, Merlot, Cabernet Sauvignon, etc.)

8 cups [2 L] low-sodium beef broth

1½ cups [360 ml] water

2 bay leaves

1 Tbsp fresh thyme leaves, roughly chopped (or ½ tsp dried thyme)

1½ tsp sugar

¾ cup [150 g] pearl barley

3 large carrots, peeled and cut into ½-in [1.5-cm] rounds

¼ cup [10 g] chopped Italian parsley, for garnish

1. Season the beef with the pepper and 1 teaspoon of the salt.

2. In a large (6-qt [6-L]) Dutch oven or soup pot, heat 1 tablespoon of the oil over medium-high heat. Add half of the beef and sear, without turning, until browned on one side, about 5 minutes (see Pro Tip). Transfer the partially browned beef to a plate. Add the remaining tablespoon of oil and the remaining beef. Sear in the same manner, and then transfer to the plate.

CONTINUED

3. Lower the heat to medium-low and add the onions, celery, and garlic. Cook, stirring frequently and scraping the brown bits off the bottom of the pot, until the vegetables are soft, about 5 minutes. Do not brown; lower the heat if necessary. (If the brown bits don't release from the bottom of the pan, help them along by adding 1 to 2 tablespoons water.)

4. Stir in the tomato paste. Add the partially browned beef (along with any juices), wine, broth, water, bay leaves, thyme, sugar, and remaining ½ teaspoon of salt to the pot; bring to a boil. Reduce the heat to low. Cover and simmer for 2 hours.

5. Remove and discard the bay leaves. Add the barley and carrots and simmer, covered, until the carrots and barley are cooked and the beef is tender, about 1 hour more. Taste and adjust the seasoning, if necessary. (I usually add a bit more salt, pepper, and sugar, but it depends on the beef broth you use.) If you like a thicker soup, simmer, uncovered, until the desired consistency is reached. For a thinner soup, add a little water. (Note: The soup might seem too "brothy" at first, but be careful not to reduce it too much because the barley quickly soaks up the broth.) Ladle into bowls, sprinkle with the parsley, and serve.

MAKE AHEAD: This soup keeps nicely in the fridge for up to 3 days, and can be frozen for up to 3 months. However, as it chills, the barley will absorb most of the broth. When you reheat it, add some water to reconstitute it— just keep in mind that you'll need to re-season it with salt and pepper as well.

open-faced bacon, avocado & pickled onion sandwich

AVOCADO TOAST HAS LONG BEEN popular, but this recipe takes it up a notch with crispy bacon and tangy pickled onions. Adding mayonnaise might seem like gilding the lily, but a little goes a long way. Serves 2

4 slices bacon

2 slices bread, preferably multigrain

1 avocado, halved and pitted

¼ tsp salt

A few grindings of freshly ground black pepper

4 tsp mayonnaise, best quality such as Hellmann's, Best Foods, or Duke's

Pickled Red Onions (recipe follows)

1. In a medium nonstick pan, lay the bacon in a single layer. Set the pan over low heat and cook until the bacon starts to buckle and curl. Use tongs or a fork to flip each slice; cook on the other side until evenly browned and crispy. Remove the bacon from the pan and drain on a paper towel–lined plate.

2. Toast the bread in the toaster or toaster oven.

3. Scoop the avocado into a bowl and mash it with the salt and pepper.

4. Spread 2 teaspoons of mayonnaise over each slice of toast. Smear the avocado on top, followed by the bacon and a scattering of pickled onions. Serve at room temperature.

CONTINUED

pickled red onions

I'M ALWAYS HAPPY to have a jar of these pickled onions in the fridge. Not only are they gorgeous, but also their sweet and tangy flavor perks up just about any dish—from sandwiches to salads to tacos. And if you're a raw onion–phobe like me, they're a great way to add onion flavor to a dish without the sharp bite of raw onion. Makes one 24-oz [680-g] jar

1 cup [240 ml] apple cider vinegar

6 Tbsp [75 g] sugar

1 Tbsp salt

1 large red onion, about 3 in [8 cm] in diameter, cut into ⅛-in [3-mm] slices

1. In a small nonreactive saucepan (see Pro Tip, page 25), bring the vinegar, sugar, and salt to a boil. Stir until the sugar and salt are dissolved. Remove the pan from the heat and add the onion to the pan. Let sit, stirring occasionally, until the onion slices are softened, 10 to 15 minutes. Transfer the onions to a medium jar and pour the vinegar mixture over the top. Press the onions down so that they are completely submerged. Let sit for at least 30 minutes before using. Cover the jar and store in the refrigerator for up to a week.

smoked gouda & pesto grilled cheese sandwiches

serve with fiery roasted-tomato basil soup (PAGE 58).

HERE'S A WAY TO MAKE grilled cheese a little more grown-up: smear the bread with pesto and fill it with smoked cheese. One lovely reader who tested the recipe for me had this to say: "Beyond awesome—especially paired with the Fiery Roasted-Tomato Basil Soup (page 58). I served it to foodie friends who proclaimed it the best grilled cheese/tomato soup combo ever." Serves 4

sourcing savvy

Most supermarkets with good cheese departments carry smoked Gouda. If you can't find it, smoked mozzarella or regular Gouda may be substituted.

pro tip

I find the cheese melts better when shredded, but it's fine to slice it very thinly if you prefer.

Eight ½-in [12-mm] slices hearty white bread, such as French or Italian

4 Tbsp [55 g] unsalted butter, at room temperature

¼ cup [60 g] homemade (page 86) or store-bought pesto

2 cups [230 g] shredded smoked Gouda cheese

1. Spread one side of each slice of bread with butter, then flip over and spread the pesto evenly over the other side of each slice (about ½ tablespoon per slice).

2. Heat a large nonstick or cast-iron skillet over medium heat. Place four slices of bread, butter-side down, in the pan. Divide the cheese evenly over the bread, then cover with a lid and cook until the cheese is about three-quarters of the way melted, a few minutes. Uncover the pan and top the sandwiches with the remaining bread, butter-side up. Flip and cook, covered, until the cheese is fully melted and the bread is golden brown, a few minutes more. Let cool slightly, then slice the sandwiches in half and serve.

the mise en place

The first term I learned in culinary school was *mise en place* (pronounced "meez-on-plass"). It's a French culinary phrase that means "put in place" and it refers to the setup required before cooking, such as prepping all of your ingredients and setting out all of your tools and equipment. For chefs, a proper mise en place is the Holy Grail. Some cooks call it their religion, and one guy I worked with even had "Mise en Place" tattooed on his arm!

In a restaurant kitchen, if your mise en place is ready, so are you. A cook might spend five hours doing prep work for a three-hour dinner service. By the time the orders roll in, the veggies are peeled, cut, and par-cooked; the sauces are made and set in a water bath on the hot line; the garlic and herbs are minced; and the meat is portioned and marinated. All that's left to do is finish the dishes *à la minute*. A proper mise en place allows restaurants to serve hundreds of diners a night from menus that offer dozens of options.

Most chefs and cookbook authors would disagree, but I don't think you need to set up a mise en place with everything sliced, diced, and measured into tiny glass bowls when cooking at home. I agree with TV chef and cookbook author Sara Moulton, who opined on her blog: "I take my life into my own hands by saying this. I'm sure all my chef instructors from my alma mater, the Culinary Institute of America, will want to shoot me at dawn. But here is what I have discovered from cooking dinner at home five or six nights a week for the last twenty-five years—mise en place (meaning, prepping and measuring all your ingredients before starting a recipe) is a waste of time, literally."

Yes, there are certain quick-cooking dishes, like stir-fries, where advance preparation is a must, but, for the most part, it's not necessary to spend a lot of time prepping ingredients before starting a recipe. I think it's generally more efficient to prep as you go, because at home, unlike in a restaurant kitchen, there's usually downtime in cooking. While the oil heats, chop the onion. While the onion cooks, mince the garlic. While the garlic cooks, season the meat. (And if ever you need more time, just take the pan off the heat.) In other words, multitask: it's the only way to get dinner done in a reasonable amount of time.

Of course, don't just wing it! I always gather all my ingredients and set them on the counter before starting a recipe. That way, I'm not scrambling to find things at the last minute, and I can be sure that I actually have everything I need. And I always read a recipe thoroughly before starting. Does the oven or grill need to be preheated? Do the butter and eggs need to be brought to room temperature? Does the meat need to marinate? Does the salad need to chill? There's nothing worse than preparing a recipe that you're about to serve, only to read that it won't be ready for another six hours.

It's good to adopt the mise en place philosophy of being prepared, but don't feel like you have to run your kitchen like a restaurant or prep like you're about to do a TV cooking demonstration. You especially don't want to create more work for yourself—all those little mise en place bowls need to be washed!

salads

My kids and husband tease me that I eat like a rabbit, which is a bit of an exaggeration. But I admit that like many women I know, I do eat a lot of salads. I suppose it's habit from years of watching what I eat, but mostly, I love to eat light and healthy.

Thankfully, gone are the days when a home-cooked meal had to consist of a protein, starch, and vegetable. I'll often make salad-as-a-meal, especially in the summertime, when I can't bear to turn on the stove and we're in the mood for something light. Other times, I'll pair a salad with a hearty soup or serve it as a side dish in place of a vegetable. After all, there are only so many dishes a person can sanely prepare on a busy weeknight. The Celery, Toasted Walnut & Pecorino Salad (page 95) and Creamy Wild Mushroom Soup (page 62) make a satisfying winter meal. And the Middle Eastern Chopped Salad (page 92) with Persian Kofta (page 141) is a great summer supper combo.

Finally, don't forget salads when you need an easy party or potluck dish. The Black Bean & Corn Salad (page 87) is my no. 1 guaranteed crowd-pleaser for a barbecue, and the Nutty Wild Rice Salad (page 99) is tailor-made for a holiday buffet.

heirloom tomato salad with burrata, pesto & pine nuts

serve with garlic & herb ciabatta (PAGE 237).

THIS IS A CAPRESE SALAD taken up a few notches, and it tastes more like a splurge than a salad. I love it as a main course in the summertime—somehow I feel that gives me carte blanche to have as much as I want. For the tomatoes, try to use a mixture of all different shapes, sizes, and colors for visual appeal. Serves 4

sourcing savvy

Burrata, meaning "buttery" in Italian, is a fresh Italian cheese made from mozzarella and cream. The outer shell is solid mozzarella, while the inside is a creamy blend of fresh mozzarella and cream. It's worth looking for (most supermarkets with good cheese sections carry it), but if you can't find it, fresh mozzarella makes a good substitute.

2 lb [910 g] tomatoes (preferably heirloom) in different colors and shapes	Two 8- to 10-oz [230- to 280-g] balls fresh burrata
¼ tsp salt	½ cup [120 g] Basil Pesto (recipe follows) or store-bought pesto
¼ tsp freshly ground black pepper	¼ cup [35 g] pine nuts, toasted (see Pro Tip)

1. Depending on the size of your tomatoes, cut some in half, some into quarters, and others into uneven chunks. Arrange on a platter and sprinkle with the salt and pepper. Cut or tear the burrata balls into chunks and arrange over the tomatoes. Dollop the pesto over the top and sprinkle with the pine nuts. Serve immediately.

CONTINUED

pro tip

To toast the pine nuts, put them in a dry skillet and cook over medium-low heat, stirring frequently, until golden in spots, about 3 minutes.

basil pesto

ONE THING I LOVE about summer cooking is stepping out the back door to pick fresh herbs from my garden. It always amazes me how the tiny seedlings that seem to take so long to sprout in May grow into more herbs than I can possibly use in August. This classic Italian pesto is the perfect way to use up a surplus of fresh basil. Makes about 1¼ cups [300 g]

⅓ cup [40 g] pine nuts or walnuts

2 large garlic cloves, roughly chopped

2 cups [80 g] packed fresh basil leaves

½ tsp salt

¼ tsp freshly ground black pepper

⅔ cup [160 ml] extra-virgin olive oil, plus more for storing

½ cup [40 g] freshly grated Parmigiano-Reggiano cheese

1. In a food processor fitted with a steel blade, put the nuts and garlic and process until coarsely chopped, about 10 seconds. Add the basil, salt, and pepper and process until the mixture resembles a paste, about 1 minute. With the processor running, slowly pour the olive oil through the feed tube and process until the pesto is thoroughly blended. Add the Parmigiano-Reggiano and process 1 minute more. Use the pesto immediately or store in a tightly sealed jar or airtight plastic container, covered with a thin layer of olive oil (the oil seals out the air and prevents the pesto from oxidizing, which would turn it an unappetizing brown color). The pesto will keep in the refrigerator for about a week or can be frozen for up to 3 months.

black bean & corn salad with chipotle honey vinaigrette

PERHAPS THE BEST COMPLIMENT this salad ever received was from one of my readers, who confessed to me, "I'm having an affair with this salad . . . please don't tell anyone." Another reader told me that she made this salad for a party, and later found one of her guests in her study, printing out copies of the recipe to hand out. It's just one of those crowd-pleasing, make-ahead recipes that everyone loves. Whether I serve it as a salad with grilled chicken or as a dip with tortilla chips (highly recommend!), the bowl is always empty and the plates are always full. Serves 6

heads up

Allow at least 1 hour for this salad to chill in the refrigerator.

FOR THE SALAD

2 ears fresh corn

1 cup [140 g] finely chopped red onion

One 15½-oz [445-g] can black beans, drained and rinsed

1 red bell pepper, seeded and diced

½ cup [10 g] loosely packed fresh cilantro leaves, chopped, plus a bit more for garnish

1 avocado

FOR THE DRESSING

2 Tbsp red wine vinegar

2 Tbsp fresh lime juice, from 1 lime

2 Tbsp honey

¼ cup plus 2 Tbsp [90 ml] vegetable oil

1 large garlic clove, roughly chopped

¾ tsp ground cumin

¾ tsp salt

¼ tsp freshly ground black pepper

¼ tsp dried oregano

2 small chipotle chiles in adobo sauce from a can

sourcing savvy

Canned chipotle chiles in adobo sauce are small dried and smoked peppers (usually red jalapeños) that come in a spicy, smoky tomato sauce. You can find them in the Latin section of most supermarkets. Once you open a can, you can transfer any remaining chiles to a plastic or glass container and store in the refrigerator for up to a month, or freeze in a sealable plastic bag for up to 6 months.

CONTINUED

1. To make the salad: Bring a large pot of salted water to a boil. Add the corn, cover, and turn the heat down to low. Simmer for 10 minutes. Remove the corn from the pot and let cool.

2. Meanwhile, place the chopped red onion in a small bowl and cover with water. Let sit for about 10 minutes, then drain completely in a sieve and set aside.

3. One at a time, holding the cooled corn upright in a large bowl, cut the kernels off the cobs in strips.

4. Add the beans, onion, bell pepper, and cilantro to the corn.

5. To make the dressing: In a blender or mini food processor fitted with the steel blade, combine all of the ingredients and process until smooth.

6. Pour the dressing over the bean and corn mixture and toss well. Cover and refrigerate for at least 1 hour or preferably overnight.

7. Right before serving, cut the avocado in half and remove the pit. Using a butter knife, cut a grid in each half. Holding each avocado half over the salad, use a spoon to scoop out the diced flesh. Toss the salad gently, then taste and adjust the seasoning, if necessary (I usually add a squeeze of fresh lime to freshen it up). Garnish with a bit of fresh chopped cilantro, if desired. Serve cold.

MAKE AHEAD: This salad is best made a day ahead of time, but wait to add the avocado until right before serving.

pro tips

When boiling corn on the cob, be sure to add enough salt that the water tastes like the sea. Try adding a few tablespoons of sugar to the water as well—you'll be amazed by how much it enhances the corn's sweetness. Or, if you don't want to steam up the kitchen, you can roast the corn following the method on page 157.

To remove the sharp taste from raw onions, soak them in cold water for about 10 minutes, then drain.

thai crunch salad
with peanut dressing

THIS RECIPE WAS INSPIRED by the popular salad served at California Pizza Kitchen. It's made with crisp napa cabbage, crunchy vegetables, and edamame, but it's the creamy peanut dressing that makes it so good. My friend Dave claims he could bathe in it! Serves 4

FOR THE THAI PEANUT DRESSING

¼ cup [65 g] creamy peanut butter

3 Tbsp vegetable oil

2 Tbsp unseasoned rice vinegar

2 Tbsp fresh lime juice, from 1 lime

2 Tbsp honey

1 Tbsp soy sauce

2½ Tbsp sugar

2 garlic cloves, roughly chopped

1-in [2.5-cm] square piece fresh ginger, peeled and roughly chopped

1 tsp salt

¼ tsp crushed red pepper flakes

2 Tbsp fresh cilantro leaves

FOR THE SALAD

4 cups [240 g] chopped napa cabbage or shredded coleslaw mix

1 cup [100 g] peeled and shredded carrots (store-bought is fine)

1 red bell pepper, seeded and cut into thin bite-sized pieces

1 small English cucumber, halved lengthwise, seeded, and thinly sliced

1 cup [150 g] cooked, shelled edamame

2 medium scallions, white and green parts, thinly sliced

½ cup [20 g] loosely packed fresh cilantro leaves, chopped

1. To make the dressing: In a blender, combine all of the ingredients except for the cilantro and blend until completely smooth. Add the cilantro and blend for a few seconds until the cilantro is finely chopped. Refrigerate until ready to serve.

2. To assemble the salad: In a large bowl, combine all of the ingredients and toss. If serving right away, drizzle the peanut dressing over the top and toss; otherwise, serve the dressing on the side so the salad doesn't get soggy.

MAKE AHEAD: The peanut dressing can be made and stored in the refrigerator up to 2 days ahead of time. The salad can be assembled, covered, and refrigerated a few hours in advance, but wait to toss the salad with the dressing until right before serving.

middle eastern chopped salad with lemon vinaigrette

KNOWN IN DIFFERENT COUNTRIES by different names, the chopped salad is a Middle Eastern staple. I was first turned on to it back in the '90s, when I was a student traveling around Israel, where the traditional "Israeli salad" is served at practically every meal, even breakfast. After having it at youth hostels, falafel stands, and restaurants, I remember thinking to myself, "It's a good thing I like this stuff!"

There are many variations of this salad, depending on the country and the cook, but the base is usually diced cucumbers and tomatoes. This version is filled out with crisp bell peppers, chickpeas, feta, and fresh mint. Serves 4 to 6

6 Tbsp [90 ml] fresh lemon juice, from 2 lemons

2 small garlic cloves, minced

2 tsp sugar

½ tsp ground cumin

1 tsp salt

¼ tsp freshly ground black pepper

½ cup [120 ml] extra-virgin olive oil

1 lb [455 g] grape tomatoes, halved

1 yellow bell pepper, seeded and diced

1 English cucumber, seeded and diced

One 15½-oz [445-g] can chickpeas, drained and rinsed

4 scallions, white and green parts, thinly sliced

⅔ cup [25 g] fresh chopped mint

6 oz [170 g] feta cheese, diced

pro tip

To seed a cucumber, cut it in half lengthwise, and then use a small spoon to scrape the seeds out.

1. In a large bowl, whisk together the lemon juice, garlic, sugar, cumin, salt, and pepper. Slowly pour in the olive oil, whisking to emulsify. Add the tomatoes, bell pepper, cucumber, chickpeas, scallions, and mint and toss well. Add the feta and toss gently to combine. Taste and adjust the seasoning, if necessary. Serve the salad immediately at room temperature or chill for up to an hour.

celery, toasted walnut & pecorino salad

LONG AGO, PROBABLY when I was a teenager, someone told me that you burn off more calories chewing celery than you do eating it. I'm pretty sure this is a myth, but it has stuck with me and I continue to find ways to eat "negative calories." I've added copious amounts of calorie-rich walnuts and cheese to this salad, which I know defeats the whole purpose, but somehow it still seems virtuous. I often make it for lunch in the wintertime. It's easy to throw together, and, even when my veggie bin is a little dull and sparse, I always seem to have a bunch of celery and a hunk of pecorino in the fridge. The salad also pairs beautifully with grilled steaks for dinner. Serves 4

¾ cup [85 g] coarsely chopped walnuts

4 cups [500 g] thinly sliced (on the bias) celery

1 cup [40 g] loosely packed fresh Italian parsley leaves, chopped

2 Tbsp finely chopped fresh chives (or substitute 1 small garlic clove, minced)

½ tsp salt

¼ tsp freshly ground black pepper

Zest of 1 lemon

2 Tbsp fresh lemon juice, from 1 lemon

⅓ cup [80 ml] vegetable oil

¾ cup [85 g] shaved or thinly sliced pecorino romano cheese

sourcing savvy

Pecorino is an Italian word meaning "from sheep's milk" and *romano* indicates that the cheese is of Roman descent, meaning it's made in Lazio, Tuscany, or Sardinia, Italy. The flavor is unmistakably sharp, strong, and piquant. If you can't find it, Parmigiano-Reggiano makes a good substitute.

1. Preheat the oven to 350°F [180°C] and set the oven rack in the middle position. Arrange the walnuts on a baking sheet in a single layer. Bake, checking frequently, until lightly toasted and fragrant, 6 to 10 minutes. Transfer to a plate and let cool.

2. In a large bowl, combine all of the ingredients except the pecorino romano. Toss well, then taste and adjust the seasoning. Add the cheese and toss gently. Transfer to a platter and serve.

arugula with roasted beets, clementines, feta & pistachios

THE FRUIT-NUT-CHEESE COMBO is always a winning formula for a salad because all of the taste and texture boxes get ticked. Here, the earthy sweetness of the beets complements the peppery bite of the arugula. On top of that, you've got creamy-tangy feta, tart-juicy clementines, and crunchy pistachios. Honey in the dressing adds a touch of sweetness that brings it all together. Not only does this salad taste great, it looks gorgeous on a platter. Serves 4

1 lb [455 g] medium beets

6 Tbsp [90 ml] extra-virgin olive oil

¼ cup [60 ml] red wine vinegar

1 Tbsp honey

1 Tbsp finely chopped shallot

½ tsp salt

¼ tsp freshly ground black pepper

5 oz [140 g] baby arugula

3 clementines, peeled and segmented

1 cup [115 g] crumbled feta cheese

⅓ cup [40 g] chopped unsalted pistachios

1. Preheat the oven to 425°F [220°C] and set an oven rack in the middle position. Wipe or scrub the beets clean, then trim the stems down to 1 in [2.5 cm], leaving the "tails" on. Place the beets on a large piece of heavy-duty aluminum foil and drizzle with 2 tablespoons of the oil. Wrap the foil around the beets to form a neat, tightly sealed packet; roast directly on the rack until tender when pierced with a knife, about 1 hour (larger beets will take longer). Unwrap the beets and let sit until cool enough to handle. Peel the beets by rubbing the skin off with a paper towel, then cut into ½-in [12-mm] wedges and place in a bowl.

2. In a large bowl, whisk together the remaining 4 tablespoons [60 ml] oil, vinegar, honey, shallot, salt, and pepper. Spoon out 2 tablespoons of the dressing and toss with the beets. Add the arugula and clementines to the remaining dressing in the bowl and toss to coat evenly. Transfer the salad to a serving platter and top with the dressed beets. Sprinkle the feta and pistachios over the top and serve immediately.

nutty wild rice salad with dried cranberries, apples & orange vinaigrette

TO ME, THIS SALAD just screams Thanksgiving potluck. It's a bit time-intensive to make as part of a whole meal, but if you're asked to bring just one special dish to a holiday party, this is the one. Not only is it make-ahead and portable, it's a welcome relief from all those other dishes that have everyone unbuttoning their pants and slipping into carb-induced food comas. Plus, it makes fabulous leftovers; just add chopped roast turkey. Serves 6

1 cup [180 g] wild rice, rinsed

1¼ tsp salt

½ tsp orange zest

¼ cup [60 ml] fresh orange juice, from 1 orange

¼ cup [60 ml] extra-virgin olive oil

3 Tbsp apple cider vinegar

2 Tbsp honey

1 tsp Dijon mustard

¼ tsp freshly ground black pepper

1 cup [110 g] pecans, toasted and coarsely chopped (see Pro Tip)

½ cup [70 g] dried cranberries

½ cup [20 g] chopped fresh Italian parsley

2 celery stalks, diced

1 tart yet sweet apple (such as Honeycrisp or Fuji), peeled, cored, and diced

¼ cup [35 g] roasted and salted pepitas (hulled pumpkin seeds)

2 scallions, light and dark green parts, thinly sliced

1. In a medium pot, combine the rice, ¾ teaspoon of the salt, and 4 cups [960 ml] of water. Bring to a boil, then turn the heat down to low; cover and simmer until the rice is tender and most of the grains have split open, 50 to 60 minutes. Transfer the rice to a fine-mesh strainer to drain any excess water. Let cool.

2. In a large bowl, whisk together the orange zest, orange juice, oil, vinegar, honey, mustard, pepper, and remaining ½ teaspoon salt. Add the cooled rice, pecans, dried cranberries, parsley, celery, apple, pepitas, and scallions. Taste and adjust the seasoning, if desired. Serve cold or at room temperature.

pro tip

To toast the pecans, preheat the oven to 350°F [180°C] and set an oven rack in the middle position. Arrange the pecans on a baking sheet and bake for 6 to 10 minutes, until toasted and fragrant.

MAKE AHEAD: This salad can be made one day ahead of time and refrigerated.

creamy grilled lemon chicken salad

heads up

Allow at least 6 hours for the chicken to marinate.

WHEN MY SON WAS BORN, I joined a "Mommy and Me" group to meet other new moms with babies the same age. Each week, we took turns hosting lunch. When it was my turn, I used to cheat and bring in prepared foods from my local gourmet market. (After all, cooking lunch for a crowd is the last thing a sleep-deprived new mother should do!) Everyone always raved about the creamy grilled chicken salad, so once the kids got older, I decided to stop paying through the nose and re-create it at home. Marinating and grilling the chicken adds so many layers of flavor, and really makes this chicken salad stand above the rest. (And, by the way, if you're looking for a good basic grilled chicken recipe, this is the one.) Serves 4 to 6

FOR THE GRILLED CHICKEN

1½ lb [680 g] boneless, skinless chicken breasts or tenderloins

¼ cup [60 ml] extra-virgin olive oil

3 large garlic cloves, minced

¼ tsp dried oregano

¾ tsp salt

½ tsp freshly ground black pepper

1 tsp lemon zest, from 1 lemon

FOR THE CREAMY DRESSING

1 cup [240 g] mayonnaise, best quality such as Hellmann's, Best Foods, or Duke's

2 tsp fresh lemon juice

1 tsp Dijon mustard

¼ tsp freshly ground black pepper

2 celery stalks, finely diced

4 scallions, light and dark green parts, thinly sliced

2 Tbsp finely chopped fresh Italian parsley

1½ tsp chopped fresh thyme or rosemary (or a combination)

Salt

CONTINUED

1. To marinate and grill the chicken: Place the chicken breasts between two pieces of wax paper and, using a meat mallet or rolling pin, pound to an even ½-in [12-mm] thickness. (Skip this step if using tenderloins.)

2. Mix all the ingredients for the marinade together in a large sealable plastic bag. Add the chicken and massage the marinade into the meat until evenly coated. Seal the bag and place in a bowl in the refrigerator to protect against leakage; let the chicken marinate for at least 6 hours or overnight.

3. Preheat a grill to high heat and lightly oil the grates. Place the chicken on the grill and cook, covered, for 2 to 3 minutes per side. Transfer to a cutting board and let cool completely, then cut into ½-in [12-mm] chunks.

4. To make the dressing: In a large bowl, whisk together the mayonnaise, lemon juice, mustard, and pepper. Add the celery, scallions, herbs, and diced chicken. Stir to combine, then taste and add salt to taste. Cover with plastic wrap and refrigerate until ready to serve.

MAKE AHEAD: This salad can be made up 2 days ahead of time and refrigerated.

sam & harry's steak salad with fennel, blue cheese & apple-walnut vinaigrette

THIS RECIPE WAS GIVEN TO ME by Michael Sternberg, one of my first mentors in the restaurant business. Michael was my boss at Sam & Harry's, a fine-dining steakhouse in Washington, D.C., that was "the place to be" back in the '90s. If you're old enough, you might remember the scene from the movie *The American President* when the character played by Michael Douglas says, "I'm gonna go to Sam and Harry's, I'm gonna order a big steak, and I'm gonna make a list of everyone who tried to [bleep] us this week!" Coincidentally, I met the real president while I was working there. But rubbing shoulders with D.C.'s movers and shakers was just one perk of the job—the other was a free lunch at the bar every day. This steak salad was one of my favorites.

The dressing for this salad is good enough to eat with a spoon, so go ahead and make extra so you'll have enough for more salads throughout the week. Serves 4

FOR THE APPLE-WALNUT VINAIGRETTE

¼ cup [30 g] walnuts

¾ cup [85 g] chopped tart-sweet apple, such as Fuji or Honeycrisp

¼ cup [60 ml] apple cider vinegar

¼ cup [60 ml] vegetable oil

1½ Tbsp chopped shallots

1 tsp Dijon mustard

1 Tbsp packed light brown sugar

¼ tsp salt

⅛ tsp freshly ground black pepper

FOR THE SALAD

½ cup [70 g] thinly sliced red onions

Two 8-oz [230-g] filet mignons

Heaping ½ tsp kosher salt

½ tsp freshly ground black pepper

1 Tbsp vegetable oil

8 cups [280 g] romaine or mixed greens

1 fennel bulb, halved, cored, and thinly sliced into half moons (about 1 cup [100 g])

⅔ cup [85 g] crumbled blue cheese

CONTINUED

sourcing savvy

Popular in Italy, fennel has a licorice-like flavor and crunchy texture. Sliced ultra-thin, it adds a fresh, cool crunch to salads. To prepare it, cut off the fennel stalks where they join the bulb (save the lacy fronds to garnish the salad, if you like). Cut the bulb in half lengthwise and remove any tough or wilted outer layers, then use the tip of a knife to remove the core in a wedge shape. Cut each half in half crosswise, and then into paper-thin half moons (if you have a mandoline slicer, this is a great recipe to use it). Fennel will dry out a bit after cutting, so if you need to cut it ahead of time, keep the slices wrapped in damp paper towels.

1. To make the vinaigrette: Preheat the oven to 350°F [180°C] and set an oven rack in the middle position. Arrange the walnuts on a baking sheet in a single layer. Bake, checking frequently, until lightly toasted and fragrant, 6 to 10 minutes. Transfer to a plate and let cool.

2. In a blender, combine the toasted walnuts with the remaining dressing ingredients and process until completely smooth.

3. To make the salad: In a bowl of cold water, submerge the onions and let soak for 10 minutes; drain and set aside.

4. Meanwhile, pat the steaks dry and, if they are thick, gently press them down so that they are about 1½ in [4 cm] tall. Season all over with the salt and pepper.

5. In a medium skillet, heat the oil over medium-high heat. When the oil is hot and shimmering, add the steaks and cook for 4 to 5 minutes on each side, turning just once, for medium-rare. Transfer the steaks to a cutting board, tent with aluminum foil, and let rest for about 5 minutes.

6. Meanwhile, in a large bowl, toss the greens with the fennel and onions. Add the dressing, little by little, until the salad is adequately dressed. Divide the lettuce mixture evenly onto serving plates.

7. Slice the steaks crosswise and arrange over or beside the salads. Sprinkle the blue cheese over the top, and pass any remaining vinaigrette on the side.

balancing flavor

Have you ever tasted a dish that was missing something but you couldn't quite figure out what it was? Oftentimes, it's as simple as adding salt (see Mastering Salt on page 51). But if you've seasoned a dish properly and it still tastes flat, it might take a little more detective work to fix it.

Start by thinking of the four most primary tastes: salty, sweet, sour, and bitter. I would also add heat, fat, and umami to the list. (*Umami* is a Japanese word that means full-bodied, meaty, and savory—think fish sauce, Parmesan cheese, and bacon.) Sometimes all of the primary tastes are used in a dish and sometimes just a few, but the best dishes have complementary flavors that balance each other.

Take the chocolate chip cookie: it's primarily sweet, but it's the bitterness of the chocolate and the salt in the background that make it irrestistible and universally loved. Or how about the margarita cocktail? It's tart and sweet, which is pleasing in itself, but it's the coarse salt on the rim of the glass that tames the bitterness of the alcohol and makes all the flavors burst.

If a dish tastes dull, think about which primary taste might be added to enhance the flavor. Rich dishes, for example, often beg for a little sourness to cut through the fat and highlight the flavors. My Open-Faced Bacon, Avocado & Pickled Onion Sandwich (page 74) would be good with the bacon and avocado alone, but it's the sweet-and-sour pickled onions that make each bite pop. My No-Churn Cheesecake Ice Cream (page 242) tasted flat until I added some sour cream, lemon juice, and a pinch of salt—now it sings with sweet, bright flavor.

Even when following a recipe, adjustments are necessary because there's so much variability in the ingredients we use. So, for example, if Brussels sprouts taste too bitter, add a touch of honey and balsamic vinegar to balance the flavor. Or if an Asian stir-fry tastes too spicy, add a squeeze of lime to cool it down. The key is to have fun, experiment, and don't worry if your dish is "off" in some way—you can almost always fix it by tweaking the primary flavors.

main courses

Making a dinner for my family, one that everyone loves, makes me happy. Never mind that I went to culinary school and cooked professionally (one would certainly hope I could whip up a good meal!), I'm still filled with pride when my family compliments my cooking and goes back for seconds. And it never gets old. I think that's true for most of us. Even my mother, for whom cooking is right up there with other fun chores like doing laundry, can't hide the glow of satisfaction when she serves up a good meal and everyone praises her cooking.

I know how hard it is to cook a meal that pleases the whole family. The chef's curse is picky eaters and, unfortunately, I am not spared. The recipes that made it into this chapter are family-pleasers because I flat-out refuse to cook separate meals for my kids. That said, I do gravitate to recipes that can be easily adjusted so that everyone will enjoy them in one form or another. For my Cedar-Planked Salmon (page 120), it's easy to leave the spices off of the kids' fillets since they prefer them plain. For my Peruvian Chicken (page 132), I make the marinade mild so the kids will eat the chicken—the heat, which Michael and I love, is in the sauce.

Many of the recipes that follow can be prepared on a busy weeknight. The others are perfect for Sundays, holidays, birthdays, or any other reason you might have to cook a special meal.

spaghetti with kale & walnut pesto

serve with celery, toasted walnut & pecorino salad (PAGE 95).

(PAGE 95).

heads up

You'll need some of the pasta cooking water for the sauce, so be sure to reserve some before you drain the pasta. It's easy to forget, so I always put a liquid measuring cup right next to the colander as a visual reminder.

pro tips

Cover the top of the food processor with plastic wrap before securing the lid; that way, you won't have to clean the top.

Toasting the walnuts isn't essential, but it brings out their flavor and makes them crunchier. Preheat the oven to 350°F [180°C]. Arrange the walnuts on a baking sheet in a single layer. Bake, checking frequently, until lightly toasted and fragrant, 6 to 10 minutes. Transfer immediately to a plate and let cool.

IF YOU LIKE KALE—OR EVEN if you're on the fence—you'll love this modern and healthy twist on pesto pasta. It's one of my go-to dinners on Friday nights. Michael loves it and I can have it on the table in 20 minutes. And if we've got a bottle of white wine chilling in the fridge, all the better to unwind after a long week. Serves 4

1 lb [455 g] spaghetti

2 cups [50 g] packed, torn kale leaves, stems removed

1 cup [20 g] tightly packed fresh basil leaves

1 tsp salt, plus more for boiling the pasta

¼ tsp freshly ground black pepper

¼ tsp sugar

½ cup [120 ml] extra-virgin olive oil

⅓ cup [40 g] walnuts, toasted if desired (see Pro Tip)

2 medium garlic cloves, roughly chopped

½ cup [50 g] grated pecorino romano cheese

FOR THE TOPPING

⅓ cup [35 g] shredded pecorino romano cheese

½ cup [60 g] chopped walnuts, toasted, if desired (see Pro Tip)

1. Bring a large pot of salted water to a boil. Add the spaghetti and boil until al dente, about 10 minutes, or according to package instructions.

2. Meanwhile, make the pesto: In the bowl of a food processor fitted with the steel blade, combine the kale and basil; process until finely chopped. Add the remaining ingredients (except the extra cheese and walnuts for the topping) and pulse until smooth.

3. Reserve 1 cup [240 ml] of the cooking water, then drain the spaghetti in a colander. Add the spaghetti back to the pot and toss with the pesto and ½ cup [120 ml] of the cooking water. If the pasta seems dry, add more of the water. Taste and adjust the seasoning, if necessary, then serve topped with the grated pecorino romano and chopped walnuts.

fusilli alfredo
(a.k.a. aunt jenn's special pasta)

A FEW YEARS AGO, my younger sister, Erica, and her husband, Guillaume, won a once-in-a-lifetime luxury vacation to Japan. I don't know what I was thinking, especially since I hadn't changed a diaper in years, but I offered to take care of my one- and two-year-old nephews so they could go (#sisteroftheyear). Boy oh boy, did those little guys give me a run for my money. When they refused to drink their bottles, I got desperate and gave them apple juice, which they had never tasted. Leo, the baby, guzzled it down with a wide two-toothed grin, and Max, the big brother, exclaimed, "I yike it!"

Much as the boys liked the apple juice, they didn't like my cooking—until I whipped up this dish, which I told them was "Aunt Jenn's Special Pasta." Think of it as shortcut mac 'n' cheese: no roux or white sauce but generous amounts of butter, cream, and cheese. It got lots of "yikes" too. Serves 4 to 6

heads up

You'll need some of the cooking water for the sauce, so be sure to reserve some before you drain the pasta.

1 lb [455 g] fusilli pasta (macaroni, farfalle, spirals, or anything you have on hand may be substituted)

½ cup (1 stick) [110 g] unsalted butter

1 cup [240 ml] heavy cream

½ cup [50 g] grated Parmigiano-Reggiano cheese

½ cup [55 g] grated fontina cheese (Gruyère, Cheddar, or any other good melting cheese may be substituted)

¼ tsp salt

¼ tsp freshly ground black pepper

1. Bring a large pot of salted water to a boil. Add the pasta and boil until al dente, about 10 minutes, or according to the package instructions. Reserve 1 cup [240 ml] of the cooking water, then drain the pasta.

2. In the same pot (no need to rinse it), melt the butter over medium-low heat. Add the cream and bring to a simmer. Add the drained pasta, ½ cup [120 ml] of the reserved pasta water, the cheeses, salt, and pepper. Stir to coat evenly, until the cheese is melted and the sauce is thickened. Add more of the reserved cooking water if the pasta seems dry; taste and adjust the seasoning with salt and pepper, if necessary. Spoon the pasta into bowls and serve.

pro tip

Don't skip salting the pasta water. The pasta will absorb the salt as it cooks, resulting in a tastier finished dish.

three-cheese white pizzas with arugula

I LOVE WHITE PIZZAS but often find them to be a little bland. Here, I boost the flavor a few ways. First, I season the dough with a few glugs of olive oil and a good dose of salt. Next, I sprinkle the dough with a combination of creamy mozzarella, tangy feta, and nutty Parmigiano-Reggiano. And, finally, I top the pizza with a lemony pile of greens. It's your main course and salad all in one, and it's loaded with flavor.

If you've never made pizza dough, it may seem a little daunting. But it comes together in just a few minutes, and then all you do is let it rise. I promise, it really is easy. Serves 4

FOR THE PIZZA DOUGH

3 cups [375 g] all-purpose flour, plus more for dusting

2 Tbsp extra-virgin olive oil

2¼ tsp (1 packet) instant, quick, or rapid-rise yeast

1¾ tsp salt

1 cup [240 ml] warm water

2 tsp cornmeal, for baking

FOR THE TOPPING

3 Tbsp extra-virgin olive oil

2 garlic cloves, finely chopped

⅓ cup [40 g] crumbled feta cheese

CONTINUED

2½ cups [280 g] shredded whole-milk mozzarella cheese (do not use low fat or part skim)

¼ cup [25 g] grated Parmigiano-Reggiano cheese

FOR THE ARUGULA SALAD

1 Tbsp fresh lemon juice, from 1 lemon

3 Tbsp extra-virgin olive oil

⅛ tsp salt

A few grinds of black pepper

5 oz [140 g] (or 4 generous handfuls) arugula

Grated Parmigiano-Reggiano cheese, for serving

If your oven has a proof setting, that's the ideal spot to let the dough rise. A sunny spot in the kitchen is also a good option.

I like to bake the crust for a few minutes before adding the cheese to ensure it gets extra crisp without over-cooking the cheese.

1. To make the pizza dough: In the bowl of a stand mixer fitted with the dough hook, combine the flour, olive oil, yeast, salt, and warm water. Mix on low speed until the dough comes together. Increase the speed to medium-low and knead until the dough is smooth and elastic, about 5 minutes. (Alternatively, you can knead the dough by hand.)

2. Transfer the dough to a lightly oiled large bowl. Cover the bowl with plastic wrap or a damp kitchen towel and let it rise in a warm, draft-free place until it has doubled in size, about 1 hour.

3. When the dough has risen, punch it down and place it on a lightly floured surface. Cut the dough in half and roll each half into a ball. Cover the dough balls with a damp kitchen towel and let them rest for 15 to 20 minutes (the dough will rise a bit).

4. Meanwhile, preheat the oven to 500°F [260°C] and set an oven rack in the lowest position. Sprinkle the cornmeal on a 13-by-18-in [33-by-46-cm] baking sheet; set aside.

5. Dust your work surface with more flour, and then press and stretch the rested dough into two 12-by-8-in [30-by-20-cm] rectangles. If the dough is sticky, dust it lightly with flour. Place the two rectangles side by side on the cornmeal-dusted baking sheet. Press the dough out again so that it almost touches the edges of the pan.

6. To make the topping: Spread the oil evenly over each dough rectangle, followed by the chopped garlic. Bake on the bottom rack of the oven for 4 minutes. Remove the pan from the oven and top each pizza with the feta, mozzarella, and Parmigiano-Reggiano (in that order). Place the pan back in the oven and bake for 6 to 8 minutes more, until the crust is golden and the cheese is melted and lightly browned in spots.

7. To make the salad: In a large bowl, whisk together the lemon juice, oil, salt, and pepper. Place the arugula in the bowl and toss to coat.

8. Transfer the pizzas to a cutting board and cut into slices. Place the slices on plates, heap the arugula salad over the top, and sprinkle with the Parmigiano-Reggiano.

MAKE AHEAD: Homemade pizza dough keeps and freezes beautifully, so go ahead and make it ahead of time or prepare a double batch. Once the dough has completed its initial rise and you've cut it in half to form two balls, lightly coat each dough ball with olive oil. Place each dough ball into its own freezer bag and seal, squeezing out all the air. Refrigerate for up to 2 days. When ready to use, let the dough sit out on the countertop for 30 minutes to warm up before stretching. You can also freeze the dough for up to 3 months. When ready to use, defrost in the refrigerator overnight (or for at least 12 hours), and then let it warm up on the countertop for about 30 minutes before stretching.

baja fish tacos

serve with chunky pea guacamole with roasted jalapeños (PAGE 28), homemade tortilla chips (PAGE 26), and black bean & corn salad with chipotle honey vinaigrette (PAGE 87).

MANY YEARS AGO, MICHAEL AND I rented a convertible and drove up the California coast. One of our favorite stops was La Jolla, where we strolled around town and stumbled upon a Mexican restaurant with great food and breathtaking views of the Pacific Ocean. I don't know if it was the scenery, the margaritas, or the fact that we were on vacation, but the fish tacos were out of this world. To recreate them at home, I came up with this version made of crispy beer-battered cod tucked into corn tortillas with a cabbage slaw and smoky chipotle sauce. I'm happy to say they come pretty darn close. Serves 4

FOR THE CABBAGE SLAW

5 cups (or one 10-oz [280-g] bag) shredded red cabbage

3 Tbsp minced red onion

½ cup [20 g] chopped fresh cilantro

3 Tbsp apple cider vinegar

1½ tsp vegetable oil

½ tsp salt

FOR THE CHIPOTLE SAUCE

¾ cup [180 g] mayonnaise, best quality such as Hellmann's, Best Foods, or Duke's

2 Tbsp fresh lime juice, from 1 lime

3 chipotle chiles in adobo sauce from a can, roughly chopped, plus 2 tsp of the sauce

1 large garlic clove, roughly chopped

FOR THE BEER BATTER

1 cup [125 g] all-purpose flour

1 tsp salt

½ tsp freshly ground black pepper

1 cup [240 ml] beer, preferably a pale lager

FOR THE FISH

Vegetable oil, for frying

1½ lb [680 g] skinless cod, cut into 1-by-4-in [2.5-by-10-cm] strips

Twelve 6-in [15-cm] soft corn tortillas, warmed

Lime wedges, for serving

sourcing savvy

The amount of chipotles called for will make a very spicy sauce. For a milder version, use just 2 chiles and 1 teaspoon of the sauce. (You can transfer any remaining chiles from the can to a sealable plastic bag and freeze them for several months.)

CONTINUED

1. To make the slaw: In a medium bowl, toss the cabbage, onion, cilantro, vinegar, oil, and salt. Set aside.

2. To make the sauce: In a blender or mini food processor fitted with the steel blade, combine the mayonnaise, lime juice, chipotles with sauce, and garlic. Blend until smooth and set aside.

3. To make the beer batter: Whisk together the flour, salt, and pepper in a medium bowl. Gradually add the beer, whisking until the batter is smooth with no lumps. Set aside.

4. To fry the fish: In a medium skillet over medium heat, add enough oil to reach a depth of ½ in [12 mm]. Heat the oil until a deep-frying thermometer registers 350°F [180°C], or when the end of a wooden spoon sizzles when dipped into the oil.

5. Working in batches so as not to crowd the pan, dip the fish strips in the beer batter and coat on both sides. Let the excess batter drip off, and then fry the fish in the hot oil until golden brown and cooked through, about 2 minutes per side. Transfer to a paper towel–lined plate to drain.

6. To assemble: Smear each tortilla with a generous amount of the chipotle sauce, and then top with the cabbage slaw. Arrange the fish on each tortilla, dividing it evenly, and serve with the lime wedges.

pro tip

There are several ways to warm corn tortillas. My favorite method is to heat them on a gas stovetop. Simply turn a gas burner on high and, using tongs, place one tortilla at a time over the burner for a few seconds, flipping once with tongs, until it's softened and beginning to char around the edges. To heat them on an electric stovetop: Place one tortilla at a time in a dry stainless-steel skillet over medium heat and cook for about 30 seconds on each side. (Note: You'll likely need a helper for either stovetop method since you'll be busy cooking the fish.)

You can also heat them in the oven: Preheat the oven to 350°F [180°C]. Make two stacks of six tortillas each and wrap each stack in aluminum foil. Bake for 15 to 20 minutes, or until heated through.

cedar-planked salmon with ancho–brown sugar spice rub

serve with roasted corn on the cob with lime-basil butter (PAGE 157), a green salad, and monterey jack & jalapeño cornbread (PAGE 232).

(PAGE 157), (PAGE 232).

heads up

While this recipe is quick and easy, be sure to plan ahead. You need to soak the cedar planks in water for at least 1 hour before cooking the salmon; otherwise they will be more prone to catching fire on the grill.

sourcing savvy

Most large supermarkets carry cedar planks near the seafood department during grilling season. They can be reused until they become overly charred. I usually get at least two dinners out of them. Scrub them clean after using and allow them to dry until their next use.

I'VE SEEN VERSIONS OF THIS DISH on countless restaurant menus, and yet it's super-easy to make at home. The cedar plank not only infuses the salmon with smoky flavor, it prevents the fish from sticking to the grill and makes an impressive presentation. One of my recipe testers called it "the perfect 'company dish' for a summer barbecue." Serves 4

1 to 2 cedar grilling planks, depending on size

1 Tbsp packed light brown sugar

¾ tsp salt

2 tsp ancho chile powder

1 tsp ground cumin

Four 6-oz [170-g] salmon fillets, skin removed

1. Fill a bowl or sink large enough to fit the cedar plank(s) with water. Soak the wood under the water for at least 1 hour.

2. Preheat the grill to medium heat. In a small bowl, combine the brown sugar, salt, chile powder, and cumin. Sprinkle the rub evenly all over the salmon fillets.

3. Place the soaked plank(s) on the grill grate, close the cover, and heat for 3 minutes. Using tongs, flip the plank(s). Place the salmon on the heated side of the plank(s). Close the grill cover and cook for 13 to 15 minutes for medium-rare, or until the desired doneness. Check occassionally and douse or mist the plank(s) with a bit of water if it catches fire. Serve on a platter right off the plank(s).

pan-seared halibut with cherry tomatoes & basil

serve with garlic & herb roasted baby potatoes (PAGE 170).

FRESH PACIFIC HALIBUT IS a seasonal splurge. It needs very little to enhance its flavor—in fact, it's almost a sin to fuss too much with it. I like to prepare it simply: pan-seared until golden and crisp with a quick sauté of sweet, garlicky cherry tomatoes on the side. Depending on how long you cook the tomatoes, they can be firm and fresh or soft and jammy. I usually aim for somewhere right in between, but they're delicious either way. Serves 4

1 pint [320 g] cherry or grape tomatoes, preferably mixed colors, halved

2 medium garlic cloves, minced

1 tsp red wine vinegar

Salt

Freshly ground black pepper

Four 6-oz [170-g] skinless Pacific halibut fillets

3 Tbsp extra-virgin olive oil

2 Tbsp chopped fresh basil

1. In a medium bowl, combine the tomatoes, garlic, vinegar, a heaping ¼ teaspoon salt, and ⅛ teaspoon pepper. Set aside.

2. Season the halibut all over with ¾ teaspoon salt and ½ teaspoon pepper.

3. Heat 2 tablespoons of the oil in a 12-in [30.5-cm] nonstick skillet over medium-high heat until hot and shimmering. Place the fish, presentation-side down, in the pan and cook, without touching, until golden brown and crisp, about 3 minutes. Flip the fish and lower the heat to medium; continue cooking until the halibut is just firm to the touch and opaque when you pry open a thicker piece with a paring knife, 3 to 4 minutes. Transfer the cooked halibut to a plate or serving platter.

4. Add the remaining 1 tablespoon oil to the pan, followed by the cherry tomato mixture. Cook, stirring occasionally, over medium heat until the tomatoes start to break down and release their juices, a few minutes. Stir in the basil, then taste and adjust the seasoning, if necessary.

5. Serve the halibut fillets with the tomatoes spooned over the top and alongside.

sourcing savvy

Pacific halibut is a firm, dense, and sweet white fish, available fresh from March into November. Avoid frozen halibut, as it tends to be dry. If you don't have access to fresh halibut, another mild white fish like haddock, mahi mahi, sea bass, tilapia, or cod may be substituted.

pro tip

Remember, when browning or searing a piece of meat or fish:

Get the pan good and hot. If the food doesn't sizzle when you place it in the oil, take it out and give the pan another minute or two to heat up.

Don't overcrowd the pan, or the temperature will drop and the food will steam instead of sear.

Resist the urge to move or flip the food before it has fully seared. It will release more easily—and, if you move it around too much, it won't develop that lovely brown color and crust.

steamed mussels with thai green curry broth

WHETHER FOR A WEEKNIGHT SUPPER or weekend soirée, mussels are a regular at our house. Not only are they easy to make, they're inexpensive, fun to eat, and elegant. They do need to be cooked immediately before serving—normally an entertaining no-no—but you can make the fragrant broth ahead of time. Come dinnertime, all that's left to do is bring the broth to a simmer and quickly steam the mussels. I always serve this dish with jasmine rice or a crusty baguette for sopping up the broth, but it never fails that someone just drinks straight from the bowl. Serves 2 to 4

sourcing savvy

Most markets sell farm-raised mussels, which are easy to clean—in fact, they are usually already cleaned and debearded. The mussels should be tightly closed. If you see a mussel that is open, tap it gently against the counter; in a live mussel, this will trigger a reaction to close its shell. If the mussel doesn't slowly close, it has died and should be discarded. Also, discard any mussels with cracked shells.

pro tip

Even though most farm-raised mussels are already quite clean, I always place them in a colander under cold running water to remove any remaining debris. If beards (the little tuft of fibers the mussel uses to connect to rocks or pilings) are present, cut or scrape them off with a paring knife or use your fingers to pull them sharply down toward the hinged point of the shells.

1 Tbsp vegetable oil

1 medium shallot, thinly sliced

1 small red bell pepper, seeded and finely diced

¼ cup [20 g] chopped scallions, white and green parts

2 garlic cloves, minced

2 Tbsp Thai green curry paste

One 14-oz [400-ml] can unsweetened coconut milk

½ cup [120 ml] water

2 Tbsp fish sauce

1 Tbsp packed light brown sugar

Zest and juice from 1 lime (about 1 tsp zest and 2 Tbsp juice)

2 lb [910 g] mussels, scrubbed and debearded

3 Tbsp chopped fresh cilantro

3 Tbsp chopped fresh Thai or Italian basil

Lime wedges, for serving

1. In a large pot, heat the oil over medium heat. Add the shallot and bell pepper and cook, stirring frequently, until soft, 3 to 5 minutes. Add the scallions, garlic, and curry paste and cook, stirring constantly, for 2 minutes more.

2. Add the coconut milk, water, fish sauce, brown sugar, lime zest, and lime juice to the pot. Bring to a boil, then taste and adjust the seasoning, if necessary.

3. Add the mussels to the broth and bring back to a gentle boil. Lower the heat to medium, cover the pot, and cook until all of the mussels are open, 3 to 4 minutes. Stir in the cilantro and basil. Spoon the mussels and broth into bowls and serve with the lime wedges.

grilled buffalo chicken kebabs

serve with basmati cilantro rice pilaf (PAGE 158) and a green salad with ranch or blue cheese dressing.

(PAGE 158)

heads up

Allow at least 6 hours for the chicken to marinate.

BOTH OF MY PARENTS ARE from Buffalo, New York, so I guess you could say I have Buffalo in my blood. Growing up, my family spent every August in a rented house on Lake Erie—visiting grandparents, aunts, uncles, and cousins, and getting our summertime fill of Buffalo's finest: Anchor Bar chicken wings, beef on weck, and Sahlen's hot dogs. This recipe is an ode to buffalo wings.

The sauce is relatively mild and family-friendly (and, by the way, kids do love this) but feel free to pump up the heat with more hot sauce or red pepper flakes if you like it spicy. Serves 4 to 6

sourcing savvy

Don't be tempted to use boneless, skinless chicken breasts in place of the chicken thighs. There's a lot of vinegar in Frank's hot sauce, and the marinade will turn lean chicken breasts to shoe leather before they even hit the grill.

FOR THE CHICKEN

¼ cup [60 ml] vegetable oil

¼ cup [60 ml] cayenne pepper sauce, such as Frank's RedHot Original (not the Buffalo flavor)

4 garlic cloves, minced

1½ tsp salt

1 tsp chili powder

1 tsp sugar

¾ tsp onion powder

¼ tsp crushed red pepper flakes

CONTINUED

3 lb [1.4 kg] boneless, skinless chicken thighs, trimmed and cut into 1½- to 2-in [3.5- to 5-cm] chunks

FOR THE BUFFALO SAUCE

6 Tbsp [85 g] unsalted butter, melted

1½ Tbsp cayenne pepper sauce, such as Frank's RedHot Original

¼ tsp crushed red pepper flakes (optional)

pro tip

Trim the fat from slippery chicken thighs with kitchen shears; it's easier than using a knife.

1. To make the chicken: In a large bowl, whisk together all of the ingredients except for the chicken. Add the chicken and stir until evenly coated. Cover the bowl with plastic wrap and marinate in the refrigerator for 6 to 10 hours (do not marinate longer, as the vinegar in the hot sauce can change the texture of the meat).

2. Line a rimmed baking sheet with aluminum foil for easy cleanup. Thread the chicken onto metal skewers (you'll need 4 to 6, depending on the size), folding if the pieces are long and thin, and place on the prepared baking sheet.

3. Preheat the grill to medium-high heat and oil the grates. Grill the chicken, covered, turning the skewers occasionally, until golden brown and cooked through, about 15 minutes. (Keep an eye on them—if they are browning too quickly, turn the heat down.) Transfer the skewers to a platter.

4. To make the sauce: Combine the melted butter, hot sauce, and red pepper flakes (if using) in a small bowl and whisk until emulsified. It will look greasy at first, but the action of the whisk should thicken the mixture into a smooth orange-colored sauce. Taste and add more hot sauce, if desired. Spoon the sauce over the kebabs or serve on the side.

smoky barbecued chicken breasts with sweet & tangy barbecue sauce

serve with black bean & corn salad with chipotle honey vinaigrette (PAGE 87) and monterey jack & jalapeño cornbread (PAGE 232).

WE HAVE A RUNNING JOKE about chicken in my family. Whenever I say we're having chicken for dinner, my husband says, "Chicken again?" and then rattles off a seemingly endless list of chicken dinners his mother used to make: "Chicken Parm, chicken cutlets, chicken stir-fry, chicken casserole, chicken pot pie" and so on. The kids jump right on the bandwagon, groaning about all my chicken dinners. What they don't realize is that this only makes me even more determined to change their minds about chicken. You could almost say I'm on a chicken crusade! Luckily, these barbecued chicken breasts always win everybody over. They are absolutely loaded with smoky barbecue flavor. Serve them with the suggested sides and I guarantee clean plates all around. Winner, winner chicken dinner! Serves 4

heads up

Allow at least 6 hours for the chicken to marinate.

1¾ lb [800 g] boneless, skinless chicken breasts or chicken tenderloins

¼ cup [60 ml] vegetable oil

3 garlic cloves, minced

1¼ tsp salt

1 Tbsp packed light brown sugar

2 tsp smoked paprika

1 tsp ground cumin

1 tsp chili powder

⅛ tsp cayenne pepper

1 cup [260 g] Sweet & Tangy Barbecue Sauce (recipe follows) or store-bought barbecue sauce

1. Place the chicken breasts between 2 pieces of wax or parchment paper and, using a meat mallet or rolling pin, pound to an even ½-in [12-mm] thickness. (Skip this step if using tenderloins.)

CONTINUED

2. In a small bowl, whisk together the oil, garlic, salt, brown sugar, smoked paprika, cumin, chili powder, and cayenne. Place the chicken in a large sealable bag. Add the marinade to the bag, press the air out, and seal. Massage the marinade into the chicken until evenly coated. Put the bag in a bowl (to protect against leakage) and place in the refrigerator to marinate for at least 6 hours or up to 24 hours.

3. Preheat the grill to high and oil the grates. Grill the chicken, covered, for 2 to 3 minutes. Flip the chicken, and then brush with some of the barbecue sauce. Cook for 2 to 3 minutes more. (Note that tenderloins will cook faster than breasts.)

4. Transfer the chicken to a serving platter and serve with remaining barbecue sauce alongside.

pro tip

There are three secrets to grilling boneless skinless, chicken breasts:

Pound the chicken to an even thickness, so the thin part doesn't dry out while the thick part finishes cooking.

Never marinate in anything acidic, like citrus juice or wine vinegar. Acids give the meat a leathery texture.

Don't overcook—when pounded thin, chicken breasts only need a few minutes per side over high heat to cook through.

sweet & tangy barbecue sauce

YOU CAN BUY A TASTY barbecue sauce at the supermarket, but it really is so easy to make your own. My kids put this sweet, tangy, smoky sauce on just about everything. Note that this recipe makes only the amount required for the Smoky Barbecued Chicken. Feel free to increase the quantities if you'd like extra; the sauce keeps well in the refrigerator for up to a week. Makes about 1 cup (260 g)

1 Tbsp vegetable oil

¼ cup [35 g] chopped yellow onion

1 garlic clove, roughly chopped

¾ cup [180 g] ketchup

¼ cup [60 ml] water

2 Tbsp packed light brown sugar

1½ Tbsp molasses

1 Tbsp apple cider vinegar

½ Tbsp Worcestershire sauce

1½ tsp chili powder

¼ tsp smoked paprika

¼ tsp ground cumin

1. In a medium saucepan, heat the oil over medium-low heat. Add the onion and garlic and cook, stirring frequently, until soft, about 5 minutes. Add the remaining ingredients and bring to a simmer. Cook, stirring occasionally, for 10 minutes more. Transfer the sauce to a blender or mini food processor fitted with the steel blade and blend until smooth.

peruvian chicken
with green sauce

serve with basmati cilantro rice pilaf (PAGE 158) and
roasted corn on the cob with lime-basil butter (PAGE 157).

heads up

Allow at least 6 hours for the chicken to marinate.

THIS IS MY TAKE ON *pollo a la brasa*, the delicious spit-roasted chicken made popular by so many Peruvian restaurants. The chicken emerges from the oven tender, juicy, and crisp-skinned. But what makes it truly special is the accompanying green sauce (recipe courtesy of my friend Kenji López-Alt, managing culinary director at Serious Eats and author of *The Food Lab*). The sauce is spicy, creamy, and downright addictive—you can put it on virtually everything, and it even makes a fabulous dip or salad dressing. Serves 4

sourcing savvy

In the poultry department, you're likely to find birds labeled "broilers," "roasters," and "fryers." These labels are based on the weight of the bird, and are meant to suggest a method of cooking. This recipe calls for a 4-lb [1.8-kg] chicken, which is typically considered a "fryer." This might seem strange since you're roasting, but don't worry about it—all of these chickens can be used in recipes interchangeably.

FOR THE CHICKEN

3 Tbsp extra-virgin olive oil

¼ cup [60 ml] fresh lime juice, from 2 limes

4 large garlic cloves, roughly chopped

1 Tbsp kosher salt

2 tsp paprika

1 tsp freshly ground black pepper

1 Tbsp ground cumin

1 tsp dried oregano

2 tsp sugar

One 4-lb [1.8-kg] whole chicken

FOR THE GREEN SAUCE

3 jalapeño peppers, seeded if desired (I use about half the seeds for a medium-hot sauce) and roughly chopped

1 cup [40 g] packed fresh cilantro leaves

2 garlic cloves, roughly chopped

½ cup [120 g] mayonnaise, best quality such as Hellmann's, Best Foods, or Duke's

¼ cup [60 g] sour cream

1 Tbsp fresh lime juice, from 1 lime

½ tsp salt

⅛ tsp freshly ground black pepper

2 Tbsp extra-virgin olive oil

CONTINUED

1. To make the chicken: In a blender or mini food processor fitted with the steel blade, combine all of the ingredients except the chicken and blend until smooth. Remove the giblets from the inside of the chicken and discard, then pat the outside of the chicken dry with paper towels; place in a bowl, breast-side up with the legs facing you. Using the handle of a wooden spoon or your fingers, loosen the skin from the flesh over the breasts and legs, being careful not to tear the skin or push all the way through (you want the marinade to stay inside the bird). Spoon about two-thirds of the marinade evenly underneath the skin, and spread the remaining one-third evenly over the skin. Marinate the chicken in the refrigerator for at least 6 hours or up to 24 hours.

2. Adjust the oven rack to the lower-middle position and preheat the oven to 425°F [220°C]. Line a roasting pan with heavy-duty aluminum foil for easy cleanup. Spray a roasting rack (preferably a V-shape) with nonstick cooking spray and place the chicken on top, breast-side up. Tie the legs together with kitchen string. Roast for 20 minutes, until the skin is golden. Turn the heat down to 375°F [190°C] and continue to roast for about an hour and 10 minutes more, or until the juices run clear when you cut between the leg and thigh. (Keep an eye on it—if it's browning too quickly, cover the bird loosely with foil.) Tent the chicken with foil and let it rest for about 20 minutes.

3. To make the sauce: In a blender or food processor fitted with the steel blade, combine all of the ingredients except the oil and blend into a smooth sauce. With the motor running, open the lid and slowly drizzle in the oil. It will seem very runny at this point, but don't worry, it will thicken up as it sits. Transfer the sauce to a bowl, cover, and refrigerate until ready to serve. The sauce will keep nicely in the refrigerator for up to 2 days.

4. To serve, tilt the chicken over the roasting pan to release the juices, then transfer to a cutting board. Carve the chicken and serve with the green sauce.

buttermilk fried chicken tenders with honey mustard sauce

serve with broccoli tots (PAGE 173).

LIKE MOST KIDS, MY DAUGHTER prefers "kid food" to "grown-up food" any day of the week. Occasionally, it works to my advantage—a trip to McDonald's makes excellent bribery—but most of the time I'm just dealing with a picky eater. Rather than desperately trying to coax her into eating dinner every night, sometimes I just make her favorites. These chicken tenders, marinated in seasoned buttermilk and pan-fried to crispy, crunchy perfection, are at the top of her list. They're delicious plain, dipped in Honey Mustard Sauce (recipe follows), or perched on top of a salad. And they're not just for picky kids: everyone loves them. Serves 4

heads up

Allow at least 4 hours for the chicken to marinate.

FOR THE MARINATED CHICKEN

2 lb [910 g] chicken tenderloins

1 cup [240 ml] buttermilk

1½ tsp salt

¼ tsp cayenne pepper

¼ tsp garlic powder

¼ tsp paprika

FOR THE BREADING

1½ cups [185 g] all-purpose flour

1½ tsp baking powder

1 heaping tsp salt

¾ tsp freshly ground black pepper

¾ tsp garlic powder

¾ tsp paprika

3 Tbsp buttermilk

3 to 4 cups [720 to 960 ml] vegetable oil, for cooking the chicken

1. To marinate the chicken: In a large sealable bag, combine the chicken tenders with the remaining marinade ingredients. Seal the bag tightly and massage the chicken until it is evenly coated with buttermilk and seasoning. Place in a bowl (in case of leakage) and refrigerate for at least 4 hours or up to 24 hours.

CONTINUED

pro tip

I find that it's hard to tell how golden the chicken is when it's immersed in the oil. It may look lightly golden, but it's actually golden brown. If you're unsure, simply pull a tender out of the oil and rest it on the paper towels to see its true color.

2. To make the breading: In a large bowl, combine the flour, baking powder, salt, pepper, garlic powder, and paprika. Whisk until well blended, then add the buttermilk and stir with a fork until the mixture is evenly clumpy.

3. Line a baking sheet with aluminum foil for easy cleanup. Remove the chicken tenders from the marinade a few at a time and toss into the breading mixture. Be sure to press the chicken firmly into the breading so clumps adhere to the meat. (It's a messy job: use one hand to remove the wet tenders from the bag and the other to toss in the breading.) Set the breaded tenders on the prepared baking sheet.

4. To fry the chicken: Line another baking sheet with a few layers of paper towels and set next to the stove. Add the oil to a large, high-sided pot until the level reaches about ¾ in [2 cm] and heat over medium-high heat until shimmering (about 350°F [180°C]). (If a cube of bread sizzles when you drop it in, it's ready.) Using tongs, place several chicken tenders in the hot oil without crowding the pan. Cook until golden brown on the bottom side, a few minutes, then flip and cook until the second side is also golden, a few minutes more. Set the cooked tenders on the paper towel–lined baking sheet to drain. Fry the remaining tenders in batches, adjusting the heat as necessary (if the tenders are browning too fast, lower the heat). Serve the tenders with honey mustard sauce.

honey mustard sauce

Makes about 1½ cups [395 g]

1 cup [240 g] mayonnaise, best quality such as Hellmann's, Best Foods, or Duke's

⅓ cup [85 g] Dijon mustard

¼ cup [85 g] honey

1 Tbsp apple cider vinegar

1. In a small bowl, whisk all of the ingredients together.

MAKE AHEAD: This sauce can be made and refrigerated up to 3 days in advance.

andouille sausage & shrimp gumbo

serve with monterey jack & jalapeño cornbread (PAGE 232), soft & fluffy pull-apart dinner rolls (PAGE 214), or a baguette for sopping up the broth.

I CAN'T CLAIM THAT this gumbo is authentic—there's not even any okra or filé powder in it—but it is delicious and easy to make, with ingredients found at your regular supermarket. And, really, there are no hard and fast rules when it comes to gumbo: each home and restaurant has its own version. The only necessity is the roux (pronounced *roo*)—or mixture of fat and flour cooked on the stove until it becomes the color of chocolate—that forms the base of the stew.

At my house, everyone always fishes out the sausage and shrimp, leaving me with a huge pot of leftover broth. If your crew does the same, feel free to increase the sausage and shrimp in the recipe. And if you have any leftover chicken in the fridge, you can throw that in too.
Serves 6 to 8

sourcing savvy

Andouille (pronounced *ahn-doo-ee*) is a seasoned and smoked sausage made from pork, most often associated with Louisiana Creole cuisine. You can usually find it in the cooked-sausage section of your supermarket—and, since it's already cooked, all you need to do is brown and heat it.

Ever wondered what the mysterious numbers are when purchasing shrimp? They're the number—usually a range—of shrimp that size that you'll get in a pound. For example, a package of large shrimp should indicate that a pound contains between 31 and 35 shrimp.

7 Tbsp [105 ml] vegetable oil

1½ lb [680 g] smoked Andouille sausage (see note, left)

¾ cup [95 g] all-purpose flour

1½ cups [210 g] chopped yellow onions

2 celery stalks, diced

1 red bell pepper, seeded and diced

7 cups [1.7 L] low-sodium chicken broth

2 Tbsp tomato paste

1 tsp salt

1 tsp sugar

¼ tsp cayenne pepper (optional)

2½ tsp Creole seasoning, such as Emeril's Essence

1 tsp chopped fresh thyme, or ½ tsp dried

2 bay leaves

1½ lb [680 g] large shrimp, peeled and deveined

½ cup [40 g] chopped scallions, white and green parts

Cooked white rice, for serving

CONTINUED

1. In a Dutch oven or large, heavy-bottomed pot, heat 1 tablespoon of the oil over medium-high heat. Add the sausages and brown on all sides, 5 to 7 minutes. Set the browned sausages aside on a cutting board.

2. Lower the heat to medium and add the remaining 6 tablespoons [90 ml] oil to the pot. Add the flour and cook, stirring slowly and constantly with a wooden spoon (making sure to scrape the corners of the pot), until the roux turns the color of milk chocolate. Depending on the type of pot you use, this process can take anywhere from 5 to 15 minutes; be patient to get the right color. (The roux will smell toasty as it browns—that's okay, but if it starts to smoke at any point, turn the heat down or remove the pot from the heat for a moment.)

3. Add the onions, celery, and bell pepper and cook with the roux, stirring frequently, until softened, 7 to 9 minutes.

4. Gradually add the chicken broth, whisking to incorporate the roux as you go, and making sure to scrape the bottom and corners of the pot. Don't worry if it looks like the roux isn't blending with the broth; it will come together once it boils.

5. Stir in the tomato paste, salt, sugar, cayenne (if using), Creole seasoning, thyme, and bay leaves. Bring to a boil, stirring frequently and scraping the bottom and corners of the pot where the roux may settle. Turn down the heat and simmer, uncovered and stirring occasionally, for 20 minutes.

6. Meanwhile, cut the browned sausages on a diagonal into ½-in [12-mm] slices.

7. Add the sliced sausage and shrimp to the gumbo and simmer until the sausage is heated through and the shrimp are just cooked, 3 to 4 minutes.

8. Remove and discard the bay leaves, and then stir in the scallions. Spoon white rice into bowls and ladle the gumbo around the rice.

MAKE AHEAD: The gumbo can be partially prepared 1 day ahead of time, through step 6. Before serving, simply bring the broth to a simmer and then proceed with the recipe.

persian kofta with tzatziki

serve with middle eastern chopped salad with lemon vinaigrette (PAGE 92) and basmati cilantro rice pilaf (PAGE 158).

ONE OF MY SON'S BEST FRIENDS is Persian, and his mom, Sougol, owns a wonderful Persian market and restaurant called Yekta, near our home. I once asked Sougol the secret to her delicious kofta, or minced beef kebabs, and she told me that they double-grind the meat in-house so that it's very fine. Since I don't have a meat grinder (and don't want to grind my own meat, to be honest), she suggested kneading it in a stand mixer. It worked like a charm! I use a few of my own tricks as well, like adding a *panade*—or mixture of bread and milk—and unflavored gelatin to make the kebabs even more tender. Serves 4 to 6

FOR THE KOFTA

¼ cup [60 ml] milk

½ cup [60 g] dried bread crumbs

½ cup [75 g] grated yellow onion, drained (see Pro Tip)

3 garlic cloves, minced

1 tsp lemon zest, from 1 lemon

1 tsp ground cumin

1½ tsp salt

¾ tsp freshly ground black pepper

2 lb [910 g] 80 percent lean ground beef

½ cup [20 g] finely chopped fresh mint

2 tsp unflavored gelatin, from 1 packet

FOR THE TZATZIKI

1½ cups [360 g] plain Greek yogurt (2 percent or whole milk)

1 medium English or hothouse cucumber, seeded, coarsely grated, and squeezed as dry as possible

2 small garlic cloves, minced

2 Tbsp extra-virgin olive oil

½ tsp salt

¼ tsp freshly ground black pepper

2 Tbsp finely chopped fresh mint

sourcing savvy

Instead of ground beef, you can use ground lamb or a combination of beef and lamb.

pro tip

To drain the grated onion, place in a fine-mesh strainer over the sink or a bowl. Using the back of a spoon, press out any excess liquid.

CONTINUED

1. To make the kofta: In a stand mixer fitted with the paddle attachment, combine the milk, bread crumbs, grated onion, garlic, lemon zest, cumin, salt, and pepper. Mix on low speed until evenly combined, about 30 seconds. Add the beef, mint, and gelatin and mix on low speed until smooth and homogenous, about 2 minutes. (I recommend using your stand mixer if you have one, but you may also use an electric hand mixer or stir by hand.)

2. Line a baking sheet with aluminum foil for easy cleanup. Divide the mixture evenly into 8 or 9 balls. Using your hands, form the balls into short sausage shapes. Insert a long metal or soaked wooden skewer vertically through each "sausage," and then use your hands to shape into a long, 1-in [2.5-cm] thick kebab. Place on the prepared baking sheet.

3. Preheat the grill to high heat and lightly oil the grates.

4. Grill the kebabs, covered, for 2 to 3 minutes per side, or until nicely browned on the exterior and no longer pink in the center. Keep a close eye on them; they are prone to flare-ups.

5. Meanwhile, to make the tzatziki: In a medium bowl, stir all of the ingredients and mix until well combined. Taste and adjust the seasoning, if necessary. Cover and chill until ready to serve.

6. Serve the grilled kebabs with the tzatziki sauce.

MAKE AHEAD: The kebabs can be formed, covered, and refrigerated 1 day ahead. They can also be frozen for up to 3 months.

juicy steakhouse burgers
(a.k.a. "segal burgers")

serve with roasted corn on the cob with lime-basil butter (PAGE 157).

(PAGE 157)

heads up

You'll notice that the recipe calls for scallions. I love them but have noticed that some children tend to pick them out. Your call.

WHO DOESN'T LOVE a big, tender, juicy steakhouse burger? Problem is, they're difficult to replicate at home because most steakhouses blend different cuts of beef—like sirloin, chuck, and short ribs—to customize the flavor and fat content of their burgers. It's certainly possible to grind your own meat or ask your butcher for a special blend, but it's not always practical. Fortunately, there's an easier way. By combining ordinary supermarket ground beef with a panade (see page 141) and lots of seasoning, you can make sensational steakhouse-style burgers in no time.

These burgers have made me a star among my children's friends. My daughter's friend Allie sweetly nicknamed them "Segal Burgers"— it stuck, and now we all call them that too. Serves 10

2 pieces white sandwich bread, crusts removed and cut into ¼-in [6-mm] pieces

⅓ cup [80 ml] milk

2½ tsp kosher salt

1 tsp freshly ground black pepper

3 garlic cloves, minced

1½ Tbsp Worcestershire sauce

2 Tbsp ketchup

3 lb [1.4 kg] 85 percent lean ground beef

3 scallions, white and green parts, thinly sliced (optional)

10 hamburger buns

Toppings of choice

pro tip

Since the panade keeps the meat tender and juicy even when overcooked, these burgers are ideal for children, the elderly, pregnant women, or anyone else who might prefer their burgers well done.

1. Preheat the grill to high heat.

2. In a large bowl, mash the bread and milk together with a fork until it forms a chunky paste. Mix in the salt, pepper, garlic, Worcestershire sauce, and ketchup.

3. Add the ground beef and scallions (if using) to the bowl and break up the meat with your hands. Gently mix everything together until just combined. Do not overmix.

4. Divide the mixture into 10 equal portions and form loose balls. Flatten the balls into patties about ¾ in [2 cm] thick and 4½ in [11 cm] in diameter. Form a slight depression in the center of each patty to prevent the burgers from puffing up on the grill.

5. Oil the grilling grates. Grill the burgers, covered, until nicely browned on the first side, 2 to 4 minutes. Flip the burgers and continue cooking for a few minutes more until the desired doneness is reached, about 3 minutes for medium-rare. Before serving, toast the buns on the cooler side of the grill, if desired.

6. Assemble and serve immediately.

MAKE AHEAD: The burgers can be formed, covered, and refrigerated up to 1 day ahead of time. They can also be frozen for up to 3 months.

valérie's steak au poivre

serve with garlic & herb roasted baby potatoes (PAGE 170) and
butter-braised brussels sprouts with shallots (PAGE 166).

WHEN I WAS TWENTY YEARS OLD, I signed up to work as a summer au pair in Paris. I went there believing I'd be visiting museums and lingering in Parisian cafés as the children scampered about me in adorable berets, always ready and willing to take a nap when I needed a break. HA! I still laugh about it to this day. Instead, I was taking care of three mischievous little boys ages two, four, and six—and a puppy—running errands, and ironing for hours on end. But the job did have one special thing going for it: my host mother, Valérie, was a wonderful cook. When I think of her today, I still picture her standing at the kitchen table, crushing peppercorns with the back of a frying pan for her steak *au poivre*—a beef tenderloin fillet with a crunchy peppercorn crust, napped with a rich Cognac sauce. Serves 4

Four 6- to 8-oz [170- to 230-g] filet mignons	⅓ cup [50 g] finely chopped shallots
1 heaping tsp kosher salt	½ cup [120 ml] Cognac or other brandy
1 Tbsp whole peppercorns	¾ cup [180 ml] heavy cream
1 Tbsp vegetable oil	1 tsp Dijon mustard
2 Tbsp unsalted butter	

1. Pat the steaks dry and, if they are thick, gently press them down so that they are about 1½ in [4 cm] thick. Season the steaks all over with the salt.

2. Seal the peppercorns inside a small plastic bag and place on a cutting board. Using a meat mallet or the bottom of a frying pan, pound the peppercorns until they are coarsely crushed. Press the crushed pepper evenly onto both sides of the steaks.

3. In a large skillet, heat the oil over medium-high heat. When the oil is hot and shimmering, add the steaks and cook for about 4 to 5 minutes on each side, turning only once, for medium-rare (or 5 to 6 minutes per side for medium). Transfer the steaks to a plate and tent with foil.

CONTINUED

4. Pour off the excess fat from the pan but do not wipe clean. Lower the heat to medium-low and add the butter and shallots. Cook, stirring constantly with a wooden spoon and scraping up the brown bits from the bottom of the pan, until the shallots are golden brown and softened, 2 to 3 minutes. Carefully add the Cognac (it may ignite) and boil, again stirring to scrape up the brown bits, until the liquid is reduced to a glaze, a few minutes longer. Add the cream and mustard and gently boil until thickened, about 3 minutes. Stir in any meat juices that accumulated on the plate holding the steaks. Transfer the steaks to serving plates and spoon the sauce over the top.

moroccan-style brisket with dried fruit & capers

serve with springtime sautéed asparagus & peas (PAGE 161) and couscous; for a gluten-free alternative to couscous, pair with cauliflower purée with thyme (PAGE 162).

FOR YEARS, I MADE Nach Waxman's "most-Googled brisket recipe" for every Jewish holiday. My family loved it, but eventually we all got tired of the same ol' same ol'. One year, I decided to mix things up a bit and give the recipe a Moroccan twist. I added Middle Eastern spices, dried fruit, and capers, and everyone thought it was a wonderful twist on the original.

The ingredient list looks long, but don't let that scare you off; it's really just a lot of spices. Plus, you can make it days ahead of time—in fact, you should, because the flavor improves the longer it sits. This dish is so abundant and impressive looking, you can keep the sides simple: some couscous and a green vegetable and your holiday dinner is done.

Serves 8

One 4- to 6-lb [1.8- to 2.7-kg] flat-cut brisket

1 heaping Tbsp kosher salt

1 tsp freshly ground black pepper

1½ Tbsp all-purpose flour

3 Tbsp vegetable oil

5 medium yellow onions, cut into slices ½ in [12 mm] thick

2 tsp packed light brown sugar

2 tsp paprika

1½ tsp ground cumin

1¼ tsp ground ginger

¾ tsp ground coriander

¾ tsp ground cinnamon

¼ tsp cayenne pepper

2 Tbsp tomato paste

5 garlic cloves, roughly chopped

6 carrots, peeled and quartered on the diagonal

14 dried apricots

12 pitted prunes

2 Tbsp capers, drained

¼ cup [10 g] chopped fresh Italian parsley

sourcing savvy

Butchers typically sell two types of brisket: flat cut and point cut. These two pieces together make up a full brisket, a large slab of muscle from the steer's chest. The point cut has more marbling, while the flat cut (also called "first cut" or "center cut") is lean but topped with a thick fat cap. This recipe calls for a flat-cut brisket. Don't let your butcher trim all the fat off! A small fat cap bastes the meat, adding flavor and keeping it from getting dry and tough. You can trim any excess fat off of the brisket and skim the fat off the gravy once it's cooked.

1. Preheat the oven to 350°F [180°C] and set an oven rack in the middle position.

CONTINUED

2. Season the brisket on both sides with the salt and pepper. Lightly dust with the flour, turning to coat both sides evenly.

3. In a heavy flameproof roasting pan or ovenproof enameled cast-iron pot just large enough to hold the brisket, carrots, and dried fruits snugly, heat the oil over medium-high heat. Add the brisket to the pan, fatty-side down, and sear until browned, 5 to 7 minutes. Using a pair of tongs and a large fork, flip the brisket over and sear the other side in the same manner.

4. Transfer the brisket to a platter, and then add the onions to the pan. (If the pan seems dry, add a few tablespoons of water.) Cook, stirring occasionally with a wooden spoon and scraping up any browned bits stuck to the bottom of the pan, until the onions are softened and golden brown, 10 to 15 minutes.

5. Add the brown sugar, paprika, cumin, ginger, coriander, cinnamon, and cayenne to the onions and cook, stirring constantly, for 1 minute more. Add 1 cup [240 ml] water and scrape up any browned bits from the bottom of the pan.

6. Remove from the heat and place the brisket, fatty-side up, and any accumulated juices from the platter on top of the onions. Spread the tomato paste evenly over the brisket, and then scatter the garlic around it. Cover the pan very tightly with heavy-duty aluminum foil or a lid, transfer to the oven, and cook for 1½ hours.

7. Carefully transfer the brisket to a cutting board (leave the oven on). Using an electric or very sharp knife, cut the meat across the grain on a diagonal into thin slices (aim for ⅛ to ¼ in [3 to 6 mm] thick). Return the slices to the pot, overlapping them at an angle so that you can see a bit of the top edge of each slice. The end result should resemble the original unsliced brisket leaning slightly backward. Scatter the carrots, apricots, prunes, and capers around the edges of the pot and baste with the sauce; cover tightly with the foil or lid and return to the oven.

8. Lower the heat to 325°F [165°C] and cook the brisket until it is fork-tender, 1¾ to 2½ hours. Transfer the brisket to a serving platter, and then sprinkle with parsley. If you're not planning to serve the brisket right away, let it cool to room temperature and then cover and refrigerate until ready to serve.

MAKE AHEAD: The brisket can be made up to 3 days ahead of time and refrigerated. Reheat the brisket in a 300°F [150°C] oven until hot, about 45 minutes. Brisket also freezes well for up to 2 months; just be sure to defrost in the refrigerator 2 days ahead of time.

pro tip

If the sauce seems greasy, transfer the meat and vegetables to a platter and cover with foil to keep warm. Pour the sauce into a bowl and let sit until the fat rises to the top. Using a small ladle, spoon out the fat. Pour the skimmed gravy back over the meat.

is it cooked? how to tell when meat, poultry & fish are done

When I was a line cook, I worked the station right next to the sauté cook. Every night, I watched in awe as he cooked dozens of beef tenderloin fillets, Chateaubriands, and lamb chops to the proper doneness—juggling an incessant stream of orders and presiding over four burners and an oven at the same time. He seemed to have a built-in timer in his head, and he could tell with a quick touch if the meat was cooked to the right temperature. The thought of working that station terrified me. And when the chef finally did give me a chance on a slow night, I went down in flames—not literally but, believe me, it wasn't pretty!

Now, even with years of professional and home cooking experience, I always rely on a meat thermometer to tell when meat is done. It's the only foolproof method—and it's no more difficult than taking a child's temperature (easier actually, since the food doesn't squirm). I have two thermometers that I use regularly: one with a leave-in probe for large roasts and an instant-read for smaller cuts of meat.

When using a thermometer, insert the probe into the thickest part of the meat (insert the thermometer horizontally for steaks, chops, and burgers). And if you're cooking meat on the bone, make sure the probe isn't touching the bone, as it could give you a false reading. Meat continues to cook while resting, and will rise another 5 to 10 degrees in temperature, so always remove it from the heat a little early. For example, if you're cooking a turkey to 165°F [75°C], take it out of the oven at 160°F [70°C]. Or if you like your steak cooked to medium, take it off the heat when it's medium-rare.

For smaller cuts of meat, like steaks or boneless chicken breasts, if you don't have a meat thermometer handy, you can make a small cut in the meat to peek. Contrary to popular belief, it will not ruin your meat. What will ruin it is if you keep it on the heat too long!

For fish, you can use a meat thermometer to test for doneness, but I think it's easier to check it the old-fashioned way. The general rule is: For every inch of thickness, fish should be cooked 8 to 10 minutes. This is a good guideline, but it's best to use visual cues as well to check for doneness. Raw fish has a translucent appearance that turns opaque and flaky once cooked. To see if it's done, poke a fork or the tip of a knife into the thickest part of the fish. The fish should be opaque and easy to pull apart. Ideally you want to catch it just before it's cooked. If the fish looks just a tad raw in the center, remove it from the heat—by the time you serve it, it'll be perfectly cooked. Of course, for some fish, like salmon, you might like it medium-rare, so remove it from the heat when it's opaque on the outside but still a little translucent in the center.

THE USDA'S RECOMMENDED SAFE MINIMUM INTERNAL TEMPERATURES ARE:

Beef, veal, lamb, and pork
(steaks and roasts): 145°F [63°C]
(with the addition of a 3-minute rest
after it reaches temperature)

Ground beef: 160°F [70°C]

Poultry: 165°F [75°C]

Fish: 145°F [63°C]

FOR COOKING BEEF TO YOUR LEVEL OF DESIRED DONENESS:

Rare: 125°F [52°C]

Medium-rare: 135°F [57°C]

Medium: 145°F [63°C]

Medium-well: 150°F [66°C]

Well-done: 160°F [71°C]

sides

On most nights, I keep my side dishes super simple. I spend most afternoons in my car shuffling my kids and their friends all over creation so, come dinnertime, I have to hit the kitchen running. I need side dishes to practically cook themselves, and they can't take longer than the main course. Fortunately for me, plain rice, buttered noodles, and instant couscous all make my children happy.

When it comes to sides, simple is usually best anyway. Not every dish on the plate needs to scream, "Look at me!" And basic side dishes make perfect complements to boldly flavored main courses. You might think the Basmati Cilantro Rice Pilaf (page 158) seems plain, but kids love it and it's the perfect match for my Grilled Buffalo Chicken Kebabs (page 126), which are loaded with spicy, salty, tangy flavor. The Springtime Sautéed Asparagus & Peas (page 161) is delicately flavored, so it makes a perfect partner to Valérie's Steak au Poivre (page 146), a peppery steak napped with a rich Cognac sauce.

Of course, side dishes don't always have supporting roles. If you're making a simple entrée, go for a side with bold flavor. The Roasted Swiss Chard (page 169) does wonders for any simple grilled steak; Curried Roasted Carrots (page 165) will elevate a basic roast chicken to a truly special meal; and the Roasted Corn on the Cob (page 157) is a showstopper that will shine next to anything you serve at a summer barbecue.

In addition to thinking about flavor when picking side dishes, remember that we eat first with our eyes: a colorful plate always looks more appetizing than a monotone one. Try to vary the textures on the plate as well. And if your main dish is rich, pair it with a light, fresh green salad.

roasted corn on the cob with lime-basil butter

WHEN COOKING CORN ON THE COB for a crowd, roasting in the husk is the way to go. The unshucked corn cooks directly on the oven rack (no dirty pans!) and the peeled-back husks make for a fun presentation. I like to brush the roasted cobs with a bright and citrusy herb butter. It brings out the sweetness of the corn and makes it taste just like summer. Serves 8

8 ears fresh corn, unshucked

½ cup (1 stick) [110 g] unsalted butter, melted

2 Tbsp finely chopped fresh basil leaves

2 Tbsp fresh lime juice, from 1 lime

Zest from 1 lime (about 1 tsp)

1 Tbsp sugar

2 tsp salt

¼ tsp cayenne pepper (optional)

sourcing savvy

Fresh corn is best cooked within a day or two of purchasing. As soon as you get home from the market, place it in a bag in the refrigerator to keep it as fresh as possible.

1. Preheat the oven to 350°F [180°C] and set an oven rack in the middle position. Place the unshucked corn directly on the oven rack and roast for 30 minutes.

2. Meanwhile, in a small bowl, mix together the melted butter, basil, lime juice and zest, sugar, salt, and cayenne, if using.

3. After removing the corn from the oven, peel down the husks. Leave the husks on to use as a handle or pull off and discard. Brush the corn with the lime-basil butter and serve.

basmati cilantro rice pilaf

IT'S HANDY TO HAVE a basic rice pilaf recipe in your repertoire, and this one goes with any number of cuisines, from Mexican to Asian to Indian. My kids think it tastes almost identical to the rice served at a certain popular chain restaurant. See if you can guess which one! Serves 6

2 Tbsp vegetable oil

⅓ cup [45 g] minced yellow onion

1 large garlic clove, minced

1½ cups [300 g] basmati rice

1 tsp salt

¼ tsp freshly ground black pepper

1 Tbsp fresh lemon juice, from 1 lemon

1 Tbsp unsalted butter

¼ cup [10 g] finely chopped fresh cilantro (or substitute Italian parsley)

pro tip

When prepared this way, it is not necessary to rinse the basmati rice before cooking.

1. In a medium saucepan, heat the oil over medium-low heat. Add the onion and cook, stirring frequently, until soft and translucent, about 5 minutes. Do not brown; lower the heat if necessary.

2. Add the garlic and rice and sauté for 2 to 3 minutes, until toasty and fragrant.

3. Add 2½ cups [600 ml] water, along with the salt and pepper; bring to a boil. Reduce the heat to low, cover, and simmer for 10 to 15 minutes, until the rice is tender and the water is absorbed. Taste the rice; if still a bit firm, add a few more tablespoons of water and cook a few minutes more.

4. Off the heat, add the lemon juice, butter, and cilantro; then mix and fluff the rice with a fork. Taste and adjust the seasoning, if necessary.

springtime sautéed asparagus & peas

THERE'S A USEFUL ADAGE: what grows together goes together. In other words, if fruits and vegetables grow in the same season and region, they'll taste great together. Think tomatoes and basil, strawberries and rhubarb, bananas and coconut, and—in this case—peas and asparagus. Plus, I always think combining vegetables in a side dish dresses them up and makes them so much more interesting. Buttered peas, for instance, are a little boring served on their own, other than perhaps to children. But the addition of asparagus, cut into pretty bite-sized lengths, transforms them into a company-worthy dish. Serves 4

2 Tbsp unsalted butter

¼ cup [40 g] minced shallots

1 bunch thin asparagus spears, ends trimmed and cut into 1½-in [4-cm] pieces on a diagonal

¼ tsp salt

Freshly ground black pepper

1 cup [120 g] frozen peas, thawed

1 tsp honey

1. In a medium saucepan, melt the butter over medium-low heat. Add the shallots and cook, stirring frequently, until soft and translucent, 4 to 5 minutes.

2. Add the asparagus, salt, and a few grinds of pepper. Continue cooking over medium-low heat, stirring frequently so the shallots don't burn, for about 5 minutes, or until tender-crisp.

3. Add the peas and honey and cook for about 1 minute more, until the peas are warmed through. Taste and adjust the seasoning, if necessary. Transfer to a platter and serve.

pro tip

When you bend an asparagus spear, it snaps at exactly the spot where the tough stalk meets the tender spear. Test one spear to see where it breaks; then, keeping the rest of the bundle together with the rubber band, cut the ends off all at once at the same spot with a sharp knife. This saves you from having to chop each one individually.

cauliflower purée with thyme

I'M NOT SURE IF IT'S just my eyes and taste buds playing tricks on me, but this cauliflower purée happens to taste remarkably like mashed potatoes. But don't make it just for that reason—it's delicious in its own right. In fact, when my friend Heather tested the recipe for me, she sent me a text that read, "OMG so good, just licked the bowl of my Cuisinart." Serves 4

1 cup [240 ml] low-sodium chicken broth

1 tsp salt

1 head cauliflower, cut into ½-in [12-mm] pieces (don't worry about keeping the florets intact)

3 Tbsp unsalted butter, cut into chunks

Freshly ground black pepper

1 tsp chopped fresh thyme

1. In a large pot, bring the chicken broth and salt to a boil. Add the cauliflower and bring back to a boil. Cover, reduce the heat to low, and steam for 20 minutes, or until the cauliflower is very tender. Use a slotted spoon to transfer the cauliflower to a food processor fitted with the steel blade. Add 3 tablespoons of the chicken broth from the pot, along with the butter, and process until smooth. Taste and adjust the seasoning with salt, if necessary, and add pepper to taste. Add the thyme and process until just combined. Scrape out the purée into a medium bowl and serve.

MAKE AHEAD: This purée can be made up to 2 days ahead of time, refrigerated, and reheated gently in the microwave or on the stovetop.

curried roasted carrots

THESE SWEET AND SPICY roasted carrots make a fabulous side dish, but they're also a treat on their own. In fact, on those rare (and dare I say treasured) nights when I'm on my own for dinner and don't feel like fussing with a full meal, I'll make them as a main course. They're like vegetable candy. Serves 4 to 6

2 lb [910 g] medium carrots, peeled and cut into thirds on the diagonal

3 Tbsp extra-virgin olive oil

1 Tbsp curry powder

½ tsp kosher salt

1 Tbsp honey, or to taste

1. Preheat the oven to 425°F [220°C] and set an oven rack in the middle position. Line a 13-by-18-in [33-by-46-cm] baking sheet with heavy-duty aluminum foil for easy cleanup.

2. Directly on the prepared baking sheet, toss the carrots with the oil, curry powder, and salt until evenly coated. Roast, stirring with a heat-proof rubber spatula a few times to prevent sticking and burning, until tender, 25 to 30 minutes.

3. Drizzle the honey over the carrots and stir to coat evenly. Taste and adjust the seasoning, if necessary. Transfer the carrots to a platter and serve.

butter-braised brussels sprouts with shallots

AROUND HOLIDAY TIME, MY INBOX fills up with inquiries about side dishes that can be prepared ahead of time. One of the most common questions is, "Can Brussels sprouts be roasted in advance?" My reply is always the same: they can, but they're nowhere near as good as they are straight out of the oven. For the holidays, when oven space is at a premium, why not braise Brussels sprouts on the stovetop a day or two ahead of time? Here, I sauté them with a heap of shallots and then simmer them in a bright broth. Right before serving, I swirl in a pat of butter, which transforms them into flavorful little cabbages you can't wait to gobble up. Serves 4

3 Tbsp unsalted butter

1 cup [150 g] thinly sliced shallots

1 lb [455 g] Brussels sprouts, trimmed but left whole

¾ cup [180 ml] low-sodium chicken broth

¾ tsp salt

¼ tsp freshly ground black pepper

1 tsp sugar

1 tsp white wine vinegar

1. In a large skillet, melt 2 tablespoons of the butter over medium heat. Add the shallots and Brussels sprouts and cook, stirring frequently, until the shallots are starting to brown and the Brussels sprouts are bright green, about 5 minutes.

2. Stir in the chicken broth, salt, pepper, and sugar; cover with a lid and lower the heat to medium-low. Simmer for 5 minutes, then remove the lid and continue simmering for 7 to 10 minutes more, stirring occasionally, until the Brussels sprouts are tender and the liquid is reduced to about ¼ cup [60 ml].

3. Stir in the remaining 1 tablespoon butter and the vinegar. Taste and adjust the seasoning, if necessary, then serve.

MAKE AHEAD: These Brussels sprouts can be made up to 2 days ahead of time, refrigerated, and then reheated gently in the microwave or on the stovetop.

roasted swiss chard with feta

SOME RECIPES ARE A total surprise. When my friend (and Once Upon a Chef right hand) Betsy Goldstein told me about this dish, I thought it seemed really odd. But I made it and before long I was texting her to say, "I'm home alone and in danger of eating this entire pan." The top layer and outer edges of the chard get crispy, almost like kale chips, while the bottom layer stays tender. But the biggest revelation is the cooked feta, which turns golden and slightly caramelized. Leftovers are delicious, too, and are even good cold, eaten standing at the fridge door. Serves 4

¾ lb [340 g] Swiss chard (green, red, yellow, or rainbow), stems chopped into slices about ½ in [12 mm] thick, leaves chopped into ribbons about 1 in [2.5 cm] wide

1 small yellow onion, halved and thinly sliced

3 Tbsp extra-virgin olive oil

Salt

Freshly ground black pepper

½ cup [55 g] crumbled feta cheese

½ tsp fresh lemon juice, from 1 lemon

heads up

Be careful with the salt: you only need about ⅛ teaspoon for the whole pan, as the feta adds plenty of salty, tangy flavor.

1. Preheat the oven to 350°F [180°C] and set an oven rack in the middle position. Line a 13-by-18-in [33-by-46-cm] baking sheet with heavy-duty aluminum foil for easy cleanup.

2. Directly on the prepared baking sheet, toss the chard stems and onion with 1 tablespoon of the oil, a pinch of salt, and a few grinds of pepper. Spread into a single layer. Bake until the chard stems have softened and the onion is just starting to brown, about 15 minutes.

3. Remove the pan from the oven and add the chard leaves on top of the stem-and-onion mixture. Drizzle with the remaining 2 tablespoons oil, a pinch of salt, and a few grinds of pepper. Using tongs, toss the leaves so that they are evenly coated. Sprinkle the feta over the top and return the pan to the oven. Bake until the stems are tender, the leaves around the perimeter of the pan are beginning to crisp, and the feta is melted and golden, about 20 minutes. Drizzle the lemon juice over the top. Taste and adjust the seasoning, if necessary, and serve.

pro tip

To easily remove the chard leaves from the stems, hold a leaf by the bottom of the stem with one hand and slide your thumb and index finger on the opposite hand up the stem to quickly separate the two.

garlic & herb roasted baby potatoes

heads up

Note that the garlic is added about midway through cooking; this prevents it from getting scorched.

THIS IS A WORKHORSE of a side dish: it's loved by all, easy to make, and goes with just about everything. The only fussy part of the recipe is arranging the potatoes cut-side down in the pan. I find that they get much crisper that way, so it's worth it. Serves 4

1½ lb [680 g] baby potatoes, halved

3 Tbsp extra-virgin olive oil

1 tsp salt

¼ tsp freshly ground black pepper

1 Tbsp chopped fresh rosemary

1 Tbsp chopped fresh thyme

5 garlic cloves, cut into halves

pro tip

If your potatoes vary in size, some may need to be cut into thirds. The idea is to make them all about the same size so that they cook evenly.

1. Preheat the oven to 425°F [220°C] and set an oven rack in the middle position.

2. Directly on a rimmed 13-by-18-in [33-by-46-cm] baking sheet (do not line the pan with foil, as the potatoes will stick), toss the potatoes with the oil, salt, pepper, half of the rosemary, and half of the thyme. Arrange the potatoes so that they are cut-side down. Roast for 15 minutes.

3. Remove the potatoes from the oven. Add the garlic and stir, scraping the potatoes up with a spatula if they are stuck to the pan (don't worry if they flip over at this point). Roast for about 20 minutes more, or until the potatoes are crisp outside and tender inside.

4. Sprinkle with the remaining herbs, then taste and adjust the seasoning, if necessary. Transfer to a platter and serve while still hot and crispy.

broccoli tots

MY KIDS LIKE BROCCOLI, which is not to say they're great eaters—they're not and I'd never jinx myself anyway—but it's one of the few vegetables they happen to like. But if you're cooking for broccoli-phobes, give these tots a try. Though they're baked in the oven, they taste strikingly similar to deep-fried tater tots, especially when dipped in ketchup.

I often make these for dinner when the kids' friends are over, and I'm always surprised by how voraciously they devour them. Who knew kids could go so wild over broccoli? Makes about 25 tots; serves 4

½ lb [230 g] broccoli, broken into florets, stems roughly chopped

⅓ cup [45 g] chopped yellow onion

½ cup [30 g] instant potato flakes

⅔ cup [75 g] grated sharp Cheddar cheese

2 eggs, beaten

Heaping ¾ tsp salt

⅛ tsp freshly ground black pepper

1 Tbsp extra-virgin olive oil

Ketchup, for serving

sourcing savvy

Instant mashed potatoes are potatoes that have been cooked, mashed, dehydrated, and made into flake form. They are typically used to make mashed potatoes, but I use them to give these tots a distinct tater tot taste.

Since this recipe only calls for a ½ pound [230 g] of broccoli, it's a great way to reinvent leftover steamed broccoli.

1. Preheat the oven to 400°F [200°C] and set a rack in the middle position.

2. Fill a medium saucepan with 1 in [2.5 cm] of water and bring to a boil. Add the broccoli and cover with a lid; reduce the heat to low and steam for 5 minutes, or until tender but still crisp. Drain well.

3. In the bowl of a food processor fitted with the steel blade, place the cooked broccoli and onion. Process until very finely chopped. Transfer the mixture to a medium bowl.

4. To the broccoli mixture, add the potato flakes, cheese, eggs, salt, and pepper. Stir until evenly combined.

5. Spread the oil onto a 13-by-18-in [33-by-46-cm] baking sheet (do not line the pan with aluminum foil, as the tots will stick). Scoop out heaping tablespoons of the broccoli mixture; squeeze the mixture in your hand to compress it, then form into tot-shaped rectangles. Arrange the tots on the baking sheet. Bake for 13 to 15 minutes, until golden brown on the bottom and firm to the touch on top. Remove the pan from the oven, then carefully flip the tots over. Return to the oven and cook until uniformly golden, 13 to 15 minutes more. Serve with ketchup.

transform vegetable scraps, stale bread, and other leftovers

When I was in culinary school, the chef instructors used to spot-check our trashcans to make sure we weren't wasting food. And let me tell you, all it takes is one time being chewed out by a French chef in front of the entire class to learn your lesson. To this day, I'm paranoid about throwing away food and have a freezer full of old bananas, vegetable scraps, and hunks of bread to prove it.

Restaurant margins are notoriously thin, so nothing is wasted in a restaurant kitchen: bones and shells are made into stocks and soups; tough cuts of meat become stew for the staff meal; cake trimmings are turned into dessert trifles; day-old bread is transformed into croutons and bread pudding; and look out for today's special—it's likely a new twist on yesterday's fish that's about to expire!

When I was a line cook, I carved countless carrots into tiny football shapes every day—the pastry chef used my scraps to make carrot cake. In cooking school, we went through dozens of egg yolks learning to make hollandaise sauce. Guess what else we learned to make that week? Yep. Meringue, pavlova, and macarons—all made with egg whites.

Put on your chef's hat next time you look around your kitchen. Is there anything lying around that could be transformed into a new dish? For this book, the dozen challahs I tested for my Braided Honey Challah (page 217) became the Baked Bourbon French Toast (page 196). And I have no less than six banana bread and muffin recipes on my website (and a few more in this book) to use up overripe bananas.

And forget about just reheating leftovers—that's a lost cause. Try to look at them as merely an ingredient for a completely different meal. Leftover Peruvian Chicken (page 132) is delicious shredded and topped with melted cheese in a quesadilla or added to Chicken Tortilla Soup (page 65). And if you have lots of bits and bobs in the fridge, you can create a salad, frittata, pasta dish, or sandwich to use them up. You can even create leftovers on purpose. If you prepare twice the pasta for tonight's main course, you'll have the base for a side dish later in the week. Or if you make a double batch of grilled chicken, you can serve it with potatoes one night, and then chop up what's left to make a Creamy Grilled Lemon Chicken Salad (page 100) for lunch.

For chefs, creativity is often born out of necessity. Instead of browsing through a cooking magazine, finding a delicious-looking recipe, and thinking: "I'll go to the store after work, get the ingredients, and follow the recipe," you might start by thinking about what's in season (and thus less expensive) or what you already have in the fridge, and then try to find a recipe for those ingredients instead.

When I was growing up, my parents nicknamed me Thumper because I was always up at the crack of dawn thumping around the house. To this day, to my husband's absolute bewilderment, I wake up every morning before the sun comes up and hop out of bed. I tiptoe downstairs to the kitchen so as not to wake the kids, brew my dark French roast coffee, check my email, and get a head start on the day. This is as much a calming ritual as it is a necessity: as soon as the clock strikes seven, the frenzied race to get the kids out the door for school begins, and I must be sufficiently caffeinated to keep my sanity.

On busy weekdays, breakfast is quick and simple: a piece of fruit with toast and jam or a bowl of Greek yogurt topped with granola. But on weekends, life with teenagers means breakfast is often the family meal of the day. Sometimes I'll make a homemade challah with scrambled eggs and bacon—or a quick dish like Savory Ham & Cheese Waffles (page 203). Believe me, the smell alone is powerful enough to lure even a slumbering 14-year-old boy out of bed. Or if I've got bananas browning on the countertop, I'll whip up a batch of Chocolate-Banana Muffins (page 192), which double as lunchbox stuffers throughout the week.

On the occasional Sunday or holiday when we've got a full house to feed, I'm grateful for breakfast recipes that can be made ahead of time. Both my Baked Bourbon French Toast (page 196) and Sausage & Cheddar Bread Pudding (page 207) can be assembled the night before, so all that's left to do in the morning is pop them in the oven.

Of course, not everyone is a morning person. If you can't fathom the idea of cooking and entertaining in the morning, don't feel constrained by the chapter title. Many of these recipes make an exceptional "BFD," or breakfast for dinner.

kale & berry breakfast smoothie

INSPIRED BY THE WONDERFUL BOOK *Kale, Glorious Kale* by Catherine Walthers, this smoothie is as good for you as it is good tasting. Strangely, you don't really taste the kale or dates, only the berries—a definite plus when serving this to children. I use frozen berries not just for convenience, but also to thicken and chill the smoothie without watering it down with ice. Makes one 1½-cup [360-ml] smoothie

1 cup [140 g] frozen blueberries

½ cup [65 g] frozen raspberries

4 pitted dates

1 cup [25 g] chopped kale (leaves only)

1 cup [240 ml] water, plus more if necessary

1. Put all of the ingredients in a blender and blend until smooth. Add a bit more water if it seems too thick. Pour into a tall glass and enjoy.

sourcing savvy

Dates are the dried fruit of the date palm tree. Here, they make a vitamin-, iron-, and potassium-rich replacement for white sugar.

stone fruit with ginger-lime syrup & fresh mint

heads up

Allow 1 hour for the syrup to cool, and at least another 45 minutes for the fruit to steep in the syrup.

I FIND IT HARD to improve on plain summer fruit—it's so perfect as is. But here, a sweet and pungent ginger syrup elevates peaches, plums, and nectarines to a whole new level. This dish is ideal for brunch, but don't rule it out as a summertime dessert, either. Serves 4

1 cup [240 ml] water

½ cup [100 g] sugar

½ cup [115 g] sliced fresh ginger, left unpeeled

¼ cup [60 ml] fresh lime juice, from 2 limes

3 ripe peaches, sliced

3 ripe plums, sliced

3 ripe nectarines, sliced

1 Tbsp chopped fresh mint

1. In a small saucepan over high heat, bring the water, sugar, and ginger to a boil. Turn the heat down to low and simmer for 10 minutes, stirring to dissolve the sugar. Strain the syrup through a fine-mesh sieve into a medium heatproof bowl; discard the ginger. Stir the lime juice into the syrup and then refrigerate until cool, about 1 hour.

2. In a shallow serving bowl, combine the sliced fruits and mint. Pour the cooled syrup over the fruit. Cover and chill for at least 45 minutes or up to a few hours. Serve the fruit and syrup in bowls with spoons.

maple, coconut & blueberry granola

FORGET BREAKFAST: THIS GRANOLA is chock-full of big crunchy clusters and perfect for snacking out of hand. I find myself inexplicably drawn to it after I fall asleep on the sofa and then wake up with a case of late-night munchies and a ravenous sweet tooth. It also makes a lovely holiday gift for neighbors and teachers, especially if you need to get it out of the house! Makes about 7 cups [800 g]

3 Tbsp pure maple syrup

3 Tbsp packed light brown sugar

⅓ cup [80 ml] vegetable oil

½ tsp ground cinnamon

½ tsp salt

2 cups [200 g] old-fashioned rolled oats (not quick-cooking or instant)

⅔ cup [75 g] roughly chopped pecans

⅔ cup [75 g] slivered almonds

⅔ cup [35 g] unsweetened shaved coconut flakes

½ cup [85 g] dried blueberries

1. Preheat the oven to 325°F [170°C] and set a rack in the upper-middle position. Line a rimmed 13-by-18-in [33-by-46-cm] baking sheet with parchment paper.

2. In a large bowl, whisk together the maple syrup, brown sugar, oil, cinnamon, and salt. Add the oats, pecans, almonds, and coconut; stir until evenly combined.

3. Transfer the mixture to the prepared baking sheet and, using a large spatula, press firmly into an even layer about ⅜ in [1 cm] thick (it won't cover the whole baking sheet). Bake for 25 to 35 minutes, until golden around the edges. Keep a close eye on it toward the end—granola can burn quickly.

4. Let cool completely on the pan, then break into large clusters and mix in the dried blueberries. Store in an airtight container for up to 2 weeks.

heads up

Be sure to add the blueberries after the granola is cooked. If you add them with the other ingredients, they'll harden in the oven.

sourcing savvy

The shaved coconut and dried blueberries—both readily available in natural-foods stores and most large supermarkets—make this granola special. However, the recipe is endlessly customizable as long as you keep the ratios the same: swap out the pecans and almonds for other nuts, or interchange the blueberries with your favorite dried fruits. (Note that shaved coconut flakes are large shards of flaked coconut; sometimes they are labeled "coconut chips" or "flaked coconut.")

peanut butter granola bars

heads up

While these bars are quick to throw together, they need a few hours to cool completely before cutting, so plan accordingly.

THESE BARS TASTE LIKE a cross between a peanut butter granola bar and a Rice Krispies Treat. What's more, unlike most homemade bars, they hold together well without crumbling. The secret ingredient is puréed dates. You can't taste the dates, but they make a sticky, nutrient-rich binder for the oats, rice cereal, and other add-ins. These bars are perfect for breakfast on the run or packing in lunchboxes—in fact, my son tells me they have high trade value in the school cafeteria. Makes 16 bars

sourcing savvy

If using large Medjool dates, you'll need 7 to 8. For smaller varieties, you'll need at least double that, if not more. Since there are so many different varieties of dates, it's best to weigh them to be sure you have the right amount.

4½ oz [130 g] pitted dates

4 Tbsp [55 g] unsalted butter

¼ cup plus 2 Tbsp [75 g] packed light brown sugar

¼ cup plus 2 Tbsp [125 g] honey

¾ cup [195 g] creamy peanut butter

¼ tsp salt

2 cups [200 g] old-fashioned rolled oats

2 cups [60 g] crispy rice cereal, such as Rice Krispies

½ cup [70 g] unsalted dry-roasted peanuts

½ cup [55 g] coarsely chopped pecans

¼ cup [25 g] flax meal, wheat germ, or wheat bran

1. Preheat the oven to 350°F [180°C] and set an oven rack in the middle position. Line a 9-by-13-in [23-by-33-cm] pan with heavy-duty aluminum foil, a big enough piece so that it hangs over the edges, and spray with nonstick cooking spray.

2. Place the dates in a food processor fitted with the steel blade. Process until finely minced and pastelike (you'll know it's ready when the mixture starts to come together into a ball).

3. In a large pot big enough to hold all of the ingredients, melt the butter over low heat. Add the puréed dates, brown sugar, honey, peanut butter, and salt; whisk until evenly combined. (You're not cooking the mixture—heating it just makes it easier to stir.) The mixture will look a little chunky; that's okay. Remove the pan from the heat and add the oats, rice cereal, peanuts, pecans, and flax meal. Use a large rubber spatula to fold the mixture until the wet ingredients evenly coat the dry ingredients.

4. Transfer the mixture to the prepared pan and, using the bottom of a glass or dry measuring cup, press firmly into an even, compact layer.

Bake for 15 to 18 minutes, until golden brown around the edges. Set the pan on a rack and let cool completely, a few hours.

5. Use the foil overhang to lift the uncut bars out of the pan and onto a cutting board. Using a large chef's knife, cut the block into 16 bars. Wrap the bars individually with foil or parchment paper for easy on-the-go snacking, or arrange them in a single layer in an airtight container. The bars will keep for several days at room temperature or up to a week in the refrigerator.

addictive almond biscotti

AN UNSUNG RECIPE FROM the blog but one of my all-time personal favorites, these biscotti were inspired by the Italian-style almond cookies served at Zuni Cafe in San Francisco. They are made by forming a fragrant, almond-studded dough into loaves, partially baking them, slicing them, and then baking them again. These are everything you want good biscotti to be: buttery, not too sweet, and crunchy but not tooth-shattering. And they're as good with your morning coffee as they are with afternoon tea, dessert wine, or ice cream. Makes 48 biscotti

sourcing savvy

Anise seeds give these biscotti a subtle licorice-like flavor that I love, even though I'm not a licorice fan. You can find anise seeds in the spice section of your supermarket, but if you don't have them, it's okay to leave them out.

2½ cups [315 g] all-purpose flour

¼ cup [35 g] yellow cornmeal

1 tsp baking powder

1 tsp salt

1 tsp anise seeds, crushed with the back of a spoon into a powder

10 Tbsp [140 g] unsalted butter

1⅓ cups [265 g] sugar

2 eggs

2 tsp vanilla extract

½ tsp almond extract

1¾ cups [200 g] slivered almonds, chopped

1. Preheat the oven to 350°F [180°C] and set the oven racks in the upper and middle thirds of the oven. Line two 13-by-18-in [33-by-46-cm] baking sheets with parchment paper.

2. In a medium bowl, whisk together the flour, cornmeal, baking powder, salt, and crushed anise seeds.

3. In the bowl of an electric mixer, cream the butter and sugar until light and fluffy, about 2 minutes. Add the eggs, one at a time, beating well after each addition and scraping down the bowl as necessary. Mix in the vanilla and almond extracts. Add the flour mixture and almonds and mix on low speed until just combined.

4. Dust your hands lightly with flour and divide the dough evenly into two disks; wrap in plastic and refrigerate for at least 15 minutes.

CONTINUED

5.   Remove the dough from the refrigerator and divide each disk into two equal pieces. Dust your hands with flour again and form each portion into a log about 2 in wide and ¾ in tall [5 cm wide and 2 cm tall] directly on the lined baking sheets. If the dough is sticky, dust your hands with more flour as necessary. Leave about 4 in [10 cm] of space between the logs to allow the dough to spread. Bake for 25 to 30 minutes, rotating the pans from top to bottom and front to back midway through, until the loaves are firm to the touch and golden around the bottom edges. Remove from the oven and let cool for 20 minutes. Leave the oven on.

6.   Once cool, transfer the logs to a cutting board. Using a serrated knife and a sawing motion, cut the logs crosswise on a diagonal into generous ½-in- [12-mm-] thick slices. They will look a little undercooked in the middle—that's okay. Arrange all the cookies, cut-side down, on one of the lined baking sheets. It will be a tight squeeze; it's not necessary to leave any space between them. Return the cookies to the oven on the middle rack and bake for 5 to 7 minutes, until lightly golden on the underside. Remove the pan from the oven, carefully flip the biscotti over, and bake for 5 minutes more, until lightly golden all over. Let the biscotti cool on the baking sheet completely before serving. The cookies will keep in an airtight container for a few weeks.

blueberry scones
with tart lemon glaze

MOST SCONES ARE DRY and crumbly, especially when left to sit out on the counter for more than a few hours. Not these. Some of the blueberries burst during baking, creating little pockets of juice that keep the scones melt-in-your-mouth tender and almost cakelike for days. The lemon glaze adds a pop of bright flavor and looks pretty, too. Makes 8 large scones

2 cups [250 g] all-purpose flour, plus more for dusting

½ cup [100 g] granulated sugar

1 Tbsp baking powder

¾ tsp salt

6 Tbsp [85 g] cold unsalted butter, cut into ½-in [1.5-cm] pieces

1 heaping cup [160 g] blueberries

⅔ cup [160 ml] heavy cream, plus 1 to 2 Tbsp more, if necessary

2 eggs

1 tsp vanilla extract

1 tsp melted butter

1 cup [100 g] confectioners' sugar

2 Tbsp fresh lemon juice, from 1 lemon

1 tsp lemon zest

1. Preheat the oven to 400°F [200°C] and set an oven rack in the middle position. Line a 13-by-18-in [33-by-46-cm] baking sheet with parchment paper.

2. In a large bowl, whisk together the flour, granulated sugar, baking powder, and salt. Add the pieces of cold butter. Use your fingertips to rub the butter into the dry ingredients until the mixture resembles coarse crumbs with pea-sized clumps of butter within. Stir in the blueberries.

3. In a small bowl, whisk together the heavy cream, 1 of the eggs, and the vanilla. Make a well in the center of the dry ingredients, then add the cream mixture. Using a rubber spatula, mix until the dough comes together. It will be a bit crumbly—that's okay. If it's too dry to come together, add 1 to 2 tablespoons more cream and mix again.

CONTINUED

heads up

These are large scones. If you prefer smaller scones, divide the dough into two rounds instead of one, and then cut each round into six wedges. Reduce the baking time to 10 to 12 minutes.

sourcing savvy

Frozen blueberries will work too, but don't defrost them or your scones will turn blue.

pro tip

When making scones, try to handle the dough as little as possible—a light hand makes for light and tender scones.

4. Dust a work surface lightly with flour; put the dough on top. Dust the dough lightly with flour, then knead gently into a ball. Press the dough into a circle about ¾ in [2 cm] high, then cut into eight wedges. It's okay if you slice through some of the blueberries.

5. Place the unbaked scones on the prepared baking sheet at least 1 in [2.5 cm] apart. Beat the remaining egg in a small bowl and use it to brush the tops of the scones (you won't use all of it). Bake for 17 to 20 minutes, until lightly golden and firm to the touch. Transfer the scones to a wire rack to cool. Slide the used parchment paper underneath the rack. (The parchment will catch any drips from the glaze.)

6. While the scones cool, make the glaze: In a small bowl, whisk together the melted butter, confectioners' sugar, and lemon juice and zest. When the scones are completely cool, drizzle the glaze over the top. (Hint: If the glaze seems too stiff to drizzle, warm it in the microwave for 5 to 10 seconds.) Let the glaze set, then serve.

MAKE AHEAD: The scone dough can be made, shaped, and refrigerated overnight and then baked directly from the fridge as directed. To freeze the dough, place the raw scones on a baking sheet until they are solid, and then transfer them to an airtight container and freeze for up to 3 months. To bake, remove the scones from the freezer while you preheat the oven. Bake as directed, but allow an extra few minutes of baking time.

chocolate-banana muffins with pecan streusel

I'VE ALWAYS FANTASIZED ABOUT owning a bakery somewhere in California, à la Meryl Streep in *It's Complicated*. Whenever I'm trying out new recipes for baked goods, I ask myself if it would go on "my" bakery menu. For these muffins, the answer is a resounding YES—especially when they're made in pretty parchment tulip liners. Makes 16 muffins

sourcing savvy

There are two types of unsweetened cocoa powder: natural (such as Hershey's) and Dutch-processed. They are not always interchangeable, so be sure to use the type that is called for in any recipe.

Parchment tulip baking cups, as pictured here, can be ordered online.

pro tip

Be sure to use mini chocolate chips; regular chips will sink to the bottom of these muffins.

1½ cups [190 g] all-purpose flour

¼ cup plus 2 Tbsp [30 g] natural unsweetened cocoa powder

1 tsp baking soda

1 tsp salt

¾ tsp ground cinnamon

½ cup (1 stick) [110 g] unsalted butter, at room temperature

1 cup [200 g] granulated sugar

2 eggs

1 tsp vanilla extract

1 cup [240 g] mashed bananas, from 2 to 3 very ripe bananas

½ cup [120 g] plain Greek yogurt or sour cream

¾ cup [130 g] mini semisweet chocolate chips

FOR THE STREUSEL

¼ cup [30 g] all-purpose flour

¼ cup [55 g] packed light brown sugar

¼ tsp ground cinnamon

2 Tbsp unsalted butter, melted

½ cup [55 g] chopped pecans

1. Preheat the oven to 375°F [190°C] and set an oven rack in the middle position. Line two muffin pans with paper liners (the recipe makes 16 muffins, so line 8 cups in each pan).

2. In a medium bowl, combine the flour, cocoa powder, baking soda, salt, and cinnamon. Whisk until there are no more lumps in the cocoa powder and the mixture is well combined.

3. In the bowl of an electric mixer, beat the butter and granulated sugar until light and fluffy, 2 to 3 minutes. Add the eggs one at a time, incorporating well after each addition. Add the vanilla, mashed bananas, yogurt, chocolate chips, and dry ingredients; mix on low speed until just combined. Do not overmix. Set aside.

4. To make the streusel: In a small bowl, stir together the flour, brown sugar, cinnamon, melted butter, and pecans. It should be crumbly.

5. Using an ice cream scoop or a large spoon, divide the batter evenly among the lined muffin pans. The cups will be almost full. Using your fingers, sprinkle the streusel topping evenly over the muffins.

6. Bake for 20 to 22 minutes, or until a toothpick inserted into the center of a muffin comes out with just a few moist crumbs attached. Let the muffins rest in the pan for about 10 minutes, and then turn them out onto a wire rack to cool completely. The muffins are best fresh, but leftovers may be stored in an airtight container at room temperature for several days.

banana pancakes

FLUFFY ON THE INSIDE, crispy on the outside, and delicately flavored with bananas and vanilla—these are amazing pancakes. The recipe, believe it or not, is adapted from Williams-Sonoma's *The Kid's Cookbook*, so you know they're simple to make. I like to top them with a heap of fresh sliced bananas to dress them up and hint at what's inside. Makes twelve 4-in [10-cm] pancakes

1½ cups [190 g] all-purpose flour

2 Tbsp sugar

2½ tsp baking powder

½ tsp salt

1 small, overripe banana (the browner, the better)

2 eggs

1 cup plus 2 Tbsp [270 ml] milk

½ tsp vanilla extract

3 Tbsp unsalted butter, melted

Unsalted butter, for frying

Vegetable oil, for frying

Pure maple syrup and sliced bananas (optional), for serving

1. In a large bowl, whisk together the flour, sugar, baking powder, and salt.

2. In a medium bowl, mash the banana with a fork until almost smooth. Whisk in the eggs. Add the milk and vanilla and whisk until well blended. Pour the banana mixture and melted butter into the flour mixture. Fold the batter gently with a rubber spatula until just blended; do not overmix. The batter should be thick and a bit lumpy.

3. Set a griddle or nonstick skillet over medium heat until hot. Put ½ tablespoon butter and 1 tablespoon vegetable oil on the griddle and swirl it around until the butter is melted. Using a 2-oz [60-ml] ladle or ¼-cup [60-g] dry measure, drop the batter onto the griddle, spacing the pancakes about 2 in [5 cm] apart. Cook until a few holes form on the top of each pancake and the undersides are golden brown, about 2 minutes. Flip the pancakes and cook until the bottoms are golden brown and the tops are puffed, 1 to 2 minutes more. Using the spatula, transfer the pancakes to a warm serving plate.

4. Wipe the griddle clean with paper towels, add more butter and oil, and repeat with the remaining batter. Serve the pancakes while still hot, topped with maple syrup and sliced bananas (if using).

baked bourbon french toast with praline topping

heads up

Allow at least 2 hours for the French toast to rest in the fridge before baking.

I CREATED THIS DISH as a fun way to use up leftover challah when I was developing my Braided Honey Challah recipe (page 217), and now I just keep making it, whether I have homemade challah in the house or not. The bottom layer is soft like bread pudding, and the top layer is golden and crisp. But the best part is the praline topping: as the pecans bubble away in the caramel sauce, they become crunchy and almost candied. File this one under over-the-top holiday brunch recipes. Serves 8

sourcing savvy

You don't need fancy bakery-quality bread; plain ol' super-market challah works just fine. If you can't find challah, brioche makes a good substitute.

Half-and-half, also known as "single cream" in the United Kingdom, is a blend of equal parts whole milk and heavy cream. If you don't have it on hand, it's fine to mix your own.

5 eggs

1⅓ cups [320 ml] half-and-half

2 Tbsp granulated sugar

1 tsp vanilla extract

4 Tbsp [60 ml] bourbon

Heaping ¼ tsp salt

One 1-lb [455-g] challah bread, cut crosswise into slices about ¾ in [2 cm] thick

½ cup (1 stick) [110 g] unsalted butter

¾ cup [160 g] packed light brown sugar

2 Tbsp light corn syrup

½ cup [55 g] chopped pecans

Pure maple syrup, for serving (optional)

1. Butter a 9-by-13-in [13-by-23-cm] baking dish (or use nonstick cooking spray).

2. In a large bowl, whisk together the eggs, half-and-half, granulated sugar, vanilla, 2 tablespoons of the bourbon, and the salt until well combined.

3. Dip each slice of challah into the custard mixture for about 5 seconds, then arrange in an overlapping pattern in the prepared baking dish. Be sure the entire bottom of the dish is covered with the bread. Pour any remaining custard evenly over the bread. Cover with plastic wrap and refrigerate for at least 2 hours or up to overnight.

4. When you're ready to cook, preheat the oven to 350°F [180°C] and set an oven rack in the middle position.

5. In a small saucepan over medium-low heat, melt the butter with the brown sugar, corn syrup, and remaining 2 tablespoons bourbon. Bring to a gentle simmer, whisking just until smooth. Stir in the pecans. Spoon the mixture evenly over the challah in the pan.

6. Cover the baking dish with aluminum foil and bake for 25 minutes. Remove the foil and continue baking until puffed and golden, about 20 minutes more. Watch closely toward the end; the pecans should be crisp but not burnt. Let cool for 10 minutes, then slice and serve warm with maple syrup, if desired.

smoked salmon spread

THERE'S A HOLE-IN-THE-WALL bagel shop that we go to whenever we visit Michael's family in New York. They make the most authentic New York bagels—big and puffy with a shiny crackled crust—and their creamy smoked salmon spread is even better. I came up with my own version of the spread so we could enjoy it at home without having to drive 250 miles. Naturally, it's great on bagels, but it also makes a delicious dip with crackers and cocktails. Now, if only I could replicate those New York bagels! Makes about 2 cups

8 oz [230 g] cream cheese

¼ cup [60 g] sour cream

¼ cup [60 g] mayonnaise, best quality such as Hellmann's, Best Foods, or Duke's

1 Tbsp fresh lemon juice, from 1 lemon

2 Tbsp capers, drained

¼ tsp Tabasco sauce

4 oz [115 g] smoked salmon, roughly chopped

2 Tbsp chopped fresh dill

2 Tbsp chopped fresh chives

Salt (optional)

1. In a food processor fitted with the steel blade, combine the cream cheese, sour cream, mayonnaise, lemon juice, capers, and Tabasco; pulse until blended. Add the salmon, dill, and chives and pulse, scraping the sides of the bowl as necessary, until the salmon is finely chopped. Taste and add salt, if necessary (I usually add about ¼ teaspoon, but it depends on the saltiness of the salmon).

MAKE AHEAD: This spread can be made up to 2 days ahead of time and refrigerated. However, it gets quite firm when cold, so let it sit out at room temperature before serving; otherwise it will be hard to spread.

creamy scrambled eggs with dill & chives

THE WAY I LEARNED to make scrambled eggs in culinary school was "low and slow" over a double boiler, which results in the creamiest, most sublime scrambled eggs you can imagine. But who wants to bother with that when there's a faster, easier way? I'm not the first to discover this trick—in fact, I pinched the idea from Food52's Genius Recipes column—but by adding a little cornstarch and milk to the eggs, you get delicate, creamy scrambled eggs and you don't have to fuss over them one bit. Serves 2 or 3

3 Tbsp milk

2 tsp cornstarch

6 eggs

Heaping ¼ tsp salt

¼ tsp dried dill

2 Tbsp unsalted butter

1 tsp finely chopped fresh chives

pro tip

Always dissolve cornstarch in a cold liquid before using it; if you add it directly to a hot liquid, it won't dissolve and you'll end up with lumps.

1. Combine the milk and cornstarch in a medium bowl. Using a fork, whisk until the cornstarch is completely dissolved and no lumps remain. Whisk in the eggs, salt, and dill.

2. In a medium nonstick skillet, melt the butter over medium heat. When the butter starts to bubble, add the egg mixture. Let it set around the edges, about 30 seconds. Using a rubber spatula, pull the edges inward, letting the runny eggs spill toward the edges of the pan. Let cook for 30 seconds more, then pull the set edges to the center again. Continue cooking, stirring constantly, until the eggs look soft and slightly under-cooked, 60 to 90 seconds more (they will continue to cook, so best not to wait until they are fully cooked to take them off the heat). Remove from the heat and transfer the eggs to a platter. Sprinkle the chives over the top and serve.

savory ham & cheese waffles

THESE WAFFLES ARE ONE OF my most-requested items for breakfast-for-dinner—or "brinner," as my kids like to call it. The batter comes together quickly. And everyone seems to enjoy the waffles in one form or another: the kids drench them with syrup; Michael dips them in mustard; and I love them with syrup and a poached egg on top. A "brinner" winner! Serves 4

2 cups [250 g] all-purpose flour

1 Tbsp sugar

1 Tbsp baking powder

1 tsp salt

3 eggs

2 cups [480 ml] milk

1 Tbsp Dijon mustard

10 Tbsp [140 g] unsalted butter, melted and slightly cooled

½ lb [230 g] thinly sliced ham, chopped

1 cup [110 g] grated sharp Cheddar cheese

Butter and pure maple syrup, for serving

1. Preheat the oven to 300°F [150°C] and set an oven rack in the middle position. Heat a waffle iron until very hot.

2. In a large bowl, whisk together the flour, sugar, baking powder, and salt.

3. In a medium bowl, whisk together the eggs, milk, and mustard. Gradually whisk the liquid mixture into the dry ingredients. Then, stir in the melted butter, ham, and cheese.

4. Coat the waffle iron with nonstick vegetable oil spray. Pour the batter onto the iron, spreading it into the corners. Cook until golden brown, 2 to 5 minutes, depending on the waffle iron. Transfer to a baking sheet and keep warm in the oven while preparing the remaining waffles. Serve with butter and warm maple syrup.

spinach & gruyère quiche

OF ALL THE SPINACH QUICHES I've tried over the years, this classic French version is my favorite. The recipe comes from my childhood friend Trish, who is not only one of the funniest people I know, but also a stunning hostess. When Trish entertains, she goes ALL out—beautiful table settings, seasonal cocktails, fabulous food, and (best of all) hilarious party games. She once created an entire game of *Jeopardy!* for our old high school gang, complete with categories like Prom Dates, '80s Pop Stars, and Senior Superlatives. This quiche is Trish's go-to brunch dish. The combination of heavy cream and Gruyère makes it insanely rich. There's also a good bit of spinach, which balances out all that richness and makes it just a little bit healthier. Serves 4 to 6

sourcing savvy

Gruyère is my first choice for this quiche—I love its nutty flavor—but if you can't find it, Cheddar may be substituted.

pro tip

Thaw frozen spinach in its package in the refrigerator a day ahead of time (place it on a plate or in a bowl to catch any leaks). If you forget, you can use the microwave or place the frozen spinach in a fine-mesh strainer and run hot water over it. No matter how you defrost it, you'll need to squeeze all the water out of the spinach. I gather it into a ball and squeeze it dry. It takes a few minutes of squeezing and re-squeezing to get all of the water out. Be patient: you want the spinach as dry as possible, otherwise your quiche will be watery.

One 9-in [23-cm] deep-dish frozen piecrust

1 Tbsp unsalted butter

½ cup [75 g] thinly sliced shallots

4 eggs

1¼ cups [300 ml] heavy cream

Pinch of ground nutmeg

¾ tsp salt

⅛ tsp cayenne pepper

1 cup [115 g] shredded Gruyère cheese

One 10-oz [280-g] package frozen chopped spinach, defrosted and wrung free of water

1. Preheat the oven to 400°F [200°C] and set an oven rack in the middle position.

2. Remove the piecrust from the freezer and thaw until just soft enough to easily prick with a fork, about 10 minutes. Prick the bottom and sides all over. Bake in its foil pan on the center rack until fully cooked and lightly golden, 10 to 15 minutes. (Keep an eye on it; if it puffs up while cooking, gently prick it with a fork so it deflates.) Remove from the oven and decrease the temperature to 325°F [170°C].

3. In a small sauté pan, melt the butter over medium-low heat. Add the shallots and cook, stirring occasionally, until soft and translucent, about 8 minutes. Do not brown. Set aside to cool.

4. In a medium bowl, whisk together the eggs, cream, nutmeg, salt, and cayenne.

CONTINUED

5. Place the cooked piecrust in its pan on a baking sheet (this makes it easy to move in and out of the oven). Spread the shallots over the bottom of the crust, and then sprinkle the shredded Gruyère on top. Scatter the spinach evenly over the cheese, breaking up the clumps as best you can, and then pour the egg mixture over the top.

6. Bake at 325°F [170°C] for 50 to 55 minutes, until the custard is set and the top is lightly golden. Serve hot or warm.

MAKE AHEAD: This quiche can be made up to a day ahead of time and refrigerated. To reheat: Cover the quiche with aluminum foil and bake in a preheated 325°F [170°C] oven for 35 to 45 minutes, or until hot in the center. The cooled quiche may also be wrapped tightly in foil and frozen for up to 2 months. Let the quiche thaw in the refrigerator overnight before reheating.

sausage & cheddar bread pudding

THIS ULTRA-RICH AND SAVORY bread pudding is one of my standbys for entertaining because it can be assembled ahead of time and feeds a crowd. The recipe was given to me by one of my oldest and dearest friends, Kelly Santoro. She got it from her friend Corey, who got it from his mother, who originally found it in an old spiral-bound church cookbook. Such is the path of a good recipe. Serves 6

heads up

Allow at least 2 hours for the bread pudding to rest in the fridge before baking.

2 Tbsp unsalted butter

1 lb [455 g] sweet or spicy pork sausage, casings removed

1 cup [140 g] chopped yellow onions

18 slices white sandwich bread, crusts removed and cut into 1-in [2.5-cm] cubes

2½ cups [285 g] shredded sharp Cheddar cheese

½ cup [20 g] chopped fresh Italian parsley

6 eggs

2 cups [480 ml] half-and-half

Scant 1 tsp salt

¼ tsp freshly ground black pepper

sourcing savvy

Some grocers sell sausage meat in bulk (or out of the casings); this makes life easier, but if you can't find it, just remove the casings. The best way is to cut the casings with kitchen shears and peel them away from the meat—this is much easier than trying to squeeze the meat out.

1. Butter a 9-by-13-in [23-by-33-cm] baking dish.

2. In a large sauté pan, melt 1 tablespoon of the butter over medium-high heat. Add the sausage and cook, stirring with a wooden spoon to break it into small clumps, until browned, about 10 minutes. Transfer the sausage to a large bowl, leaving the fat in the pan.

3. Lower the heat to medium and add the onions and the remaining 1 tablespoon butter to the pan. Cook the onions, stirring constantly, until soft and translucent, about 5 minutes. Add the onions to the bowl with the sausage, along with the bread cubes, cheese, and parsley. Toss well, then spread the mixture evenly in the prepared baking dish.

CONTINUED

4. In a medium bowl, whisk together the eggs, half-and-half, salt, and pepper.

5. Pour the custard evenly over the bread and sausage mixture. Cover tightly with plastic wrap and refrigerate for at least 2 hours or up to overnight.

6. Preheat the oven to 350°F [180°C] and set an oven rack in the middle position. Bake for about 1 hour, until puffed and golden brown. Slice into squares and serve immediately.

cheats to keep you sane when you're feeding a crowd

One of the women in my book club once asked me for advice on what to cook for one of those roving neighborhood dinner parties, where each course is served at a different house. She explained that fifty people were coming to her house for the main course portion of the meal, and that she was cooking to impress. I went into a minor panic at the thought of it, and told her she was very brave! I would *never* cook dinner for fifty people all by myself—even if someone else were taking care of appetizers and dessert.

Michael and I have hosted our fair share of large gatherings over the years, including an annual father-son fantasy football draft party. Every year, I'm faced with the same dilemma: what on earth am I going to feed all my son's friends and their fathers, plus all of the siblings and significant others who come along? I love to cook, but I know I'll lose my sanity if I try to make everything myself, so I always bring in some part of the meal. Believe it or not, that usually ends up being less expensive, and it's a huge load off my mind knowing that part of the meal—sometimes even the main course—is being delivered to my door.

I like this way of entertaining. I think of my job as putting together the pieces of a great meal, not necessarily as the wearied cook who has to make every single little thing. The key is knowing what to make yourself and what to buy. Most restaurants or markets do one thing really well, and that's what you should order. For instance, French women don't usually bother making complicated desserts because there's an extraordinary patisserie on every street corner selling gorgeous confections that would be way too time-consuming to bake at home.

There's a barbecue joint near us that makes the most amazing St. Louis–style dry rub ribs. The ribs are far superior to anything I could make at home because I don't own a smoker. For a casual party, I like to order a few dozen racks and then make all the sides myself. How easy is that?

I'll even admit that I've ordered my Thanksgiving turkey on occasion. Let's be honest: can I really make a turkey that much tastier than the gourmet market in town? I do make my own gravy and sides—my family might revolt if I didn't—but not having to worry about the bird and all the oven space it takes up sure takes the pressure off on Thanksgiving day.

There's no shame in getting "a little help." I find that as long as the food is good, the drinks are flowing, and the music is playing, no one cares who cooked the food. And, as long as you make a few things yourself, you'll still feel all the pride for having served a memorable meal.

breads

I know it may seem like a ridiculous idea to bake your own bread, especially when life is busy and there's a bakery down the street. But making homemade bread, whether a sweet braided challah (page 217) or a crusty walnut rye (page 225), is extraordinarily satisfying. In fact, I would say that in the realm of home cooking, the smell of bread baking in the oven, filling the house with warmth and goodness, trumps all. And making it is not the least bit hard; it just requires time, patience, and a little practice.

That said, I know baking yeast bread is neither for everyone nor for every day. Many of the recipes in this chapter are quick breads, which do not rely on yeast and can be thrown together right before supper. That's right: you can get cornbread, biscuits, and savory scones in the oven in 15 minutes and they can do double-duty as a starch. And more effort doesn't necessarily mean better results: my family's favorite recipe in this chapter is the Garlic & Herb Ciabiatta (page 237) made from a store-bought loaf—it's the quickest and easiest of the bunch.

soft & fluffy pull-apart dinner rolls

WHEN MY EDITOR, Amy Treadwell, suggested I include a dinner roll recipe in this chapter, I set to work testing dozens of recipes. While many were quick and easy with short rising times—a plus, for sure— they were also disappointingly bland and dense. I finally came up with this recipe, which uses instant potato flakes and nonfat dried milk to tenderize the bread and add flavor. These rolls are soft and fluffy, with an open crumb and rich, buttery flavor. Though they're not the fastest dinner rolls out there, I believe they are the very best. Makes 12 rolls

½ cup [120 ml] milk

1 egg

2 cups [250 g] all-purpose flour, plus more for dusting

½ cup [30 g] instant potato flakes

2 Tbsp nonfat dried milk

2½ Tbsp sugar

1¼ tsp instant, quick, or rapid-rise yeast

1¼ tsp salt

4 Tbsp [55 g] unsalted butter, at room temperature, plus more for serving

1. In a small microwave-safe bowl, combine the milk and ¼ cup [60 ml] water. Heat until lukewarm, 20 to 30 seconds on high heat. (This can also be done in a small saucepan on the stove.)

2. In the bowl of an electric mixer fitted with the dough hook, combine the egg, flour, potato flakes, dried milk, sugar, yeast, salt, and 3 table-spoons of the butter. Add the warm milk and water mixture and knead on medium-low speed for about 5 minutes until you have a smooth, soft dough. (Don't worry if the dough sticks a bit to the bottom of the bowl.) To remove the dough from the bowl, dust your hands with flour and scrape it out.

3. Using your hands (dust them with more flour if necessary), shape the dough into a ball and place in a lightly greased bowl. Cover the bowl with plastic wrap or a damp kitchen towel and let the dough rise in a warm, draft-free place until it's doubled in bulk, about 90 minutes.

CONTINUED

4.	Invert the dough onto a lightly floured work surface (it will deflate). Divide it into 12 even pieces (each piece should weigh 1¾ to 2 oz [50 to 55 g]). Shape each piece of dough into a smooth ball by tucking and pinching the edges underneath to form a plump little bun.

5.	Grease a 9-in [23-cm] round baking pan with nonstick cooking spray. Place the rolls in the pan, arranging 8 evenly around the perimeter and 4 in the center. Cover the pan with plastic wrap or a damp kitchen towel and let the rolls rise until they're almost doubled in bulk, puffy, and touching, about 1 hour. Toward the end of the rising time, preheat the oven to 350°F [180°C] and set an oven rack in the middle position.

6.	Melt the remaining 1 tablespoon butter. Brush the rolls with the melted butter and bake for 23 to 25 minutes, until golden brown. Remove from the oven and turn out onto a wire rack. Serve warm or at room temperature with butter. Store the rolls in a sealable plastic bag for several days at room temperature, or freeze for longer storage (see Make Ahead).

MAKE AHEAD: To freeze the baked rolls, let them cool completely, wrap tightly in aluminum foil, and place in a freezer bag. Freeze for up to 1 month. To thaw: Remove the rolls from the freezer and let thaw at room temperature for at least 3 hours. Place the foil-wrapped rolls in a preheated 350°F [180°C] oven for 10 to 15 minutes, until warm.

braided honey challah

CHALLAH IS THE BREAD of celebration in Jewish tradition, but I put it in the matzo ball soup and bagel category: it appeals to everyone. It's a rich, slightly sweet loaf with a shiny golden crust and pillowy interior. But what makes it truly special is its distinctive braid, which symbolizes, among other things, the joining together of family and friends.

Rest assured, challah looks like far more trouble than it actually is. Think of it as a once-in-a-while baking therapy project. Kneading and braiding the dough, smelling the challah baking in the oven—it really is satisfying. And when the long braided loaf is presented at the dinner table, it is a sight to behold.

I owe much of the credit for this recipe to Nancy Hirschorn, one of my lovely readers, who has been perfecting her challah recipe for over thirty-five years. Thank you, Nancy, for all the pointers. Makes one 16-in [40-cm] loaf (about 16 slices)

4¼ cups [530 g] all-purpose flour, plus more for dusting

1 Tbsp instant, quick-, or rapid-rise yeast

2 tsp salt

¾ cup [180 ml] lukewarm water

6 Tbsp [90 ml] vegetable oil

6 Tbsp [130 g] honey

3 eggs

1 egg yolk

1. In a stand mixer fitted with the dough hook, combine the flour, yeast, and salt. Mix on low speed for 30 seconds to combine. In a separate bowl, combine the lukewarm water, oil, honey, 2 of the whole eggs, and the egg yolk. Add to the dry ingredients and knead on medium-low speed until you have a soft, tacky dough that clings to the bottom of the bowl, 5 to 7 minutes. The dough may seem sticky, but have faith—it's supposed to be.

CONTINUED

heads up

This recipe makes one 16-in [40-cm] loaf, which is much longer than a store-bought challah. It's huge! You can cut the recipe in half and make one smaller loaf, but the presentation isn't nearly as dramatic. And, honestly, I wouldn't worry about having leftovers—stale challah makes incredible French toast (see the Baked Bourbon French Toast with Praline Topping on page 196) or bread pudding.

sourcing savvy

Instant yeast is not the same as active dry yeast—it rises faster and does not need to be dissolved in liquid. Note that the quantity required for this recipe is more than one packet.

pro tips

When baking yeast breads, rising times are only a guide; the temperature in your kitchen, the humidity level outdoors, and how you knead the dough will all affect the rising time.

If you like, sprinkle poppy or sesame seeds onto the unbaked challah after brushing it with the egg wash.

2. Dust your hands generously with flour, then scrape the sticky, elastic dough out onto a lightly floured work surface. Dust the top of the dough lightly with flour and knead into a soft, smooth ball. Lightly grease a large bowl with oil or nonstick cooking spray. Place the dough in the bowl, flip it over once so the top is lightly oiled, and then cover the bowl with plastic wrap. Allow the dough to rise in a warm, draft-free spot until it's puffy and doubled in size, 1½ to 2½ hours.

3. Invert the dough onto a lightly floured work surface and dust with flour. It will deflate. Use the pictorial guide on page 219 to cut the dough into 4 even pieces, and then stretch and roll each piece into a rope about 20 in [50 cm] long. Lay the ropes parallel to one another (vertically). Pinch them together at the top, and then fan them out. If the ropes shrink a bit, just work them back into their original length.

4. Braid the strands. Pinch the ends together and tuck them under to create a nice shape. Begin by taking the strand farthest to the right and weave it toward the left through the other strands using this pattern: over, under, over. Take the strand farthest to the right and repeat the weaving pattern again: over, under, over. Repeat this pattern, always starting with the strand farthest to the right, until the whole loaf is braided.

5. Carefully transfer the braided loaf to a parchment-lined 13-by-18-in [33-by-46-cm] baking sheet. Cover the loaf loosely with plastic wrap and let it rise in a warm, draft-free spot until puffy, 60 to 90 minutes. Toward the end of the rising time, preheat the oven to 350°F [180°C] and set an oven rack in the middle position. (Note that the loaf will continue to rise significantly in the oven.)

6. In a small bowl, beat the remaining egg and brush the beaten egg generously over the risen dough. Bake for 30 to 35 minutes, until the crust is a rich brown color and the internal temperature is between 190°F [88°C] and 200°F [95°C] on an instant-read thermometer. Remove the bread from the oven and place it on a wire rack to cool. Challah is best enjoyed fresh, but leftovers will keep for a few days in a sealed plastic bag.

MAKE AHEAD: Challah can be baked, cooled, tightly wrapped, and frozen for up to 3 months. Allow it to thaw at room temperature for at least 3 hours before serving.

cinnamon swirl bread

I MUST HAVE GONE THROUGH twenty pounds of flour creating this recipe. Believe me, no one complained. My house smelled like Cinnabon for days, and the kids were happy to have cinnamon bread for breakfast, lunch, and, yes, even dinner. The challenge was that I could never get the bread quite sweet or cinnamon-y enough. And the more filling I added, the more the loaf wanted to unravel when sliced. After many trials, I finally figured out the secret to securing the swirl: confectioners' sugar. The cornstarch in the sugar acts as a glue that holds the layers together. Finally, a tall and fluffy loaf with a lavish cinnamon swirl! This bread is wonderful warm out of the oven but even better the next day, toasted and smeared with salted butter. Makes 1 loaf (about twenty ½-in [12-mm] slices)

heads up

Be sure to use a 9-by-5-in [23-by-12.5-cm] loaf pan; an 8-by-4-in [20-by-10-cm] pan is too small.

4 cups (500 g) all-purpose flour, plus more for dusting

2¼ tsp (1 packet) instant, quick-, or rapid-rise yeast

2 tsp salt

6 Tbsp [75 g] granulated sugar

1 cup [240 ml] lukewarm milk (110° to 115°F [38° to 43°C])

6 Tbsp [85 g] unsalted butter, melted

3 eggs

¾ cup [85 g] confectioners' sugar

3 Tbsp ground cinnamon

1. In the bowl of a heavy-duty electric mixer fitted with the dough hook, combine the flour, yeast, salt, and granulated sugar. Mix on low speed to combine. Add the warm milk, melted butter, and 2 of the eggs; mix on low speed until well combined, about 1 minute. Increase the speed to medium-low and knead for 7 minutes. The dough will be very elastic and sticky—that's good!

2. Generously dust your hands with flour and scrape the dough out onto a clean, lightly floured work surface. Lightly dust the top of the dough with flour and shape into a soft, smooth ball.

CONTINUED

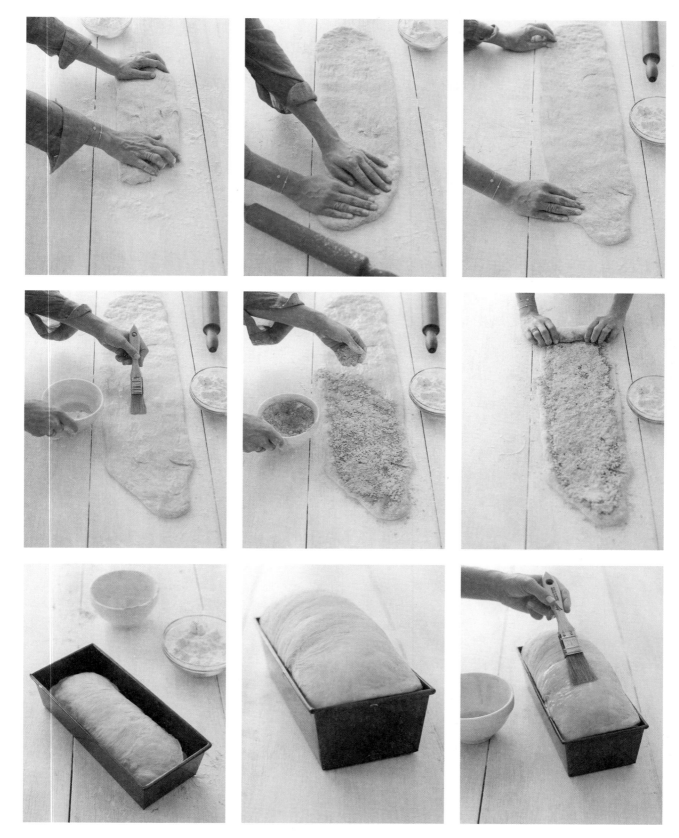

3. Grease a large bowl with oil or nonstick cooking spray. Place the dough in the bowl and flip it over once so the top is lightly oiled. Cover the bowl with plastic wrap or a damp kitchen towel and let the dough rise in a warm, draft-free spot until doubled in size, 1 ½ to 2 hours.

4. Meanwhile, in a medium bowl, whisk together the confectioners' sugar and cinnamon. Set aside.

5. When the dough has risen, dust a large, clean work surface with flour (you'll need a space of about 3 ft [1 m]). Dump the sticky dough onto the work surface and turn it a few times to coat it with flour so that you can handle it. It should come together into a soft, workable dough. Dust your work surface lightly with flour again; then, using your hands, press the dough into a 6-by-32-in [15-by-80-cm] rectangle. (Feel free to use a rolling pin if that's easier for you.)

6. In a small bowl, beat the remaining egg. Brush the dough with the beaten egg (don't use it all; you'll need some for brushing the top of the loaf before baking). Sprinkle the cinnamon-sugar mixture evenly over the top. Use it all, even though it seems like too much. Starting at one end, roll the dough very tightly into a thick log, keeping it very neat and compact. Pinch the seam tightly together. (See pictorial guide on page 223.)

7. Spray a 9-by-5-in [23-by-12.5-cm] loaf pan with nonstick cooking spray. Place the rolled dough in the pan, seam-side down. Loosely cover with plastic wrap or a damp kitchen towel and let rise in a warm, draft-free spot until the center of the dough crests about 1 in [2.5 cm] over the top of the pan, 45 minutes to 1 hour.

8. Toward the end of the rising time, preheat the oven to 350°F [180°C] and set a rack in the lower third of the oven. Brush the loaf with the remaining beaten egg and bake for 35 to 40 minutes, until it is golden brown and the temperature in the middle of the loaf is between 190°F [88°C] and 200°F [95°C] on an instant-read thermometer. Let the loaf cool in the pan for about 5 minutes, then run a butter knife around the edges to loosen. Turn the loaf out onto a rack and let cool completely before slicing.

MAKE AHEAD: This bread can be baked, cooled, tightly wrapped, and frozen for up to 3 months. Allow it to thaw at room temperature for at least 3 hours before serving.

salt-crusted currant & walnut rye bread

I FIRST LEARNED TO BAKE this bread in culinary school, and I've been baking it ever since—for nearly twenty years. I've tweaked the recipe quite a bit over time, but the original idea comes from Chef Patrick O'Connell's timeless and wonderful *The Inn at Little Washington Cookbook*. The loaves are wonderful for breakfast with softened butter and a drizzle of honey. And they're equally good as a cocktail bread, sliced thin and topped with cheese—or with gravlax, honey mustard, and red onions. The loaves freeze beautifully. Makes 2 long loaves (about sixty ¼-in [6-mm] slices)

heads up

Note that this recipe calls for two different kinds of salt. Table salt is used to flavor the dough, while kosher salt is used to add flavor and crunch to the crust.

¾ cup [80 g] rye flour

2¼ cups [280 g] all-purpose flour, plus more for dusting

1¼ tsp table salt (or fine sea salt)

2¼ tsp (1 packet) instant, quick-, or rapid-rise yeast

2 tsp sugar

2 Tbsp caraway seeds

2 Tbsp unsalted butter, at room temperature

1¼ cups [300 ml] warm water

1 cup [140 g] dried currants

¾ cup [85 g] chopped walnuts

1 egg, beaten, for brushing

1 tsp kosher salt

sourcing savvy

Rye flour can be found in the baking aisle of most large supermarkets.

1. In the bowl of an electric mixer fitted with the dough hook, combine the rye flour, all-purpose flour, table salt, yeast, sugar, and 1½ tablespoons of the caraway seeds. Briefly mix on low speed to combine, and then add the butter and warm water. Knead on medium-low speed for 5 minutes. The dough will look shaggy at first, and then it will get quite sticky before coming together into a tacky dough that clings a bit to the bottom of the bowl. Add the currants and walnuts and knead on low speed for 1 to 2 minutes more to incorporate.

CONTINUED

2. Dust a work surface with all-purpose flour. Scrape the dough onto the work surface and knead a few times with your hands to ensure the currants and walnuts are mixed in evenly. Place the dough in a lightly oiled bowl and flip it over once so the top is lightly oiled. Cover with plastic wrap or a damp kitchen towel, and allow the dough to rise in a warm, draft-free place until doubled in size, 1 to 2 hours.

3. Line a 13-by-18-in [33-by-46-cm] baking sheet with parchment paper. On a lightly floured work surface, cut the dough in half and shape into two 14-by-2-in [35-by-5-cm] loaves. Cover with plastic wrap or a damp kitchen towel and let rise in a warm, draft-free place until the loaves have expanded by about 1 in [2.5 cm], 30 to 45 minutes.

4. Meanwhile, preheat the oven to 350°F [180°C] and set an oven rack in the middle position.

5. Brush the loaves with the beaten egg and sprinkle evenly with the remaining ½ tablespoon caraway seeds and the kosher salt. Lift the parchment up toward the loaves to shake any loose caraway seeds and salt onto the sides of the loaves.

6. Bake for about 35 minutes, or until the loaves are golden brown and the internal temperature is between 190°F [88°C] and 200°F [95°C] on an instant-read thermometer. Transfer the loaves to a wire rack and let cool before slicing.

MAKE AHEAD: This bread can be baked, cooled, tightly wrapped, and frozen for up to 3 months. Allow it to thaw at room temperature for at least 3 hours before serving.

almost southern buttermilk biscuits

SOUTHERN BISCUIT RECIPES typically call for White Lily flour, a low-protein brand primarily available in the southern U.S. states that makes for ultra-tender, melt-in-your-mouth biscuits. I can't find White Lily flour easily where I live, so I use a blend of all-purpose flour and cornstarch to get the same effect. These biscuits are rich and buttery in flavor with a fluffy interior and toasty golden crust. Plus, they're easy to make. You can throw the dough together in 10 minutes and enjoy the biscuits with your dinner less than 15 minutes later. Makes 12 biscuits

sourcing savvy

If you'd rather not buy a whole carton of buttermilk for this recipe, it's easy to make your own. Simply add 2½ teaspoons of lemon juice or white vinegar to a liquid measuring cup. Then, add milk to the ¾-cup [180-ml] line and let sit for 10 to 15 minutes, or until slightly thickened and curdled.

2 cups [250 g] all-purpose flour, plus more for dusting

3 Tbsp cornstarch

1 Tbsp baking powder

¼ tsp baking soda

1 Tbsp sugar

1¼ tsp salt

10 Tbsp [140 g] cold unsalted butter, cut into ½-in [12-mm] chunks

¾ cup [180 ml] buttermilk

1. Preheat the oven to 425°F [220°C] and set an oven rack in the middle position. Line a 13-by-18-in [33-by-46-cm] baking sheet with parchment paper.

2. In the bowl of a food processor fitted with the steel blade, combine the flour, cornstarch, baking powder, baking soda, sugar, and salt. Pulse a few times to mix. (Alternatively, whisk the ingredients together in a large bowl.)

3. Add the butter and pulse until the mixture resembles coarse sand with a few pea-sized clumps of butter intact. (If making by hand, "cut" the butter into the dough with a pastry cutter or two knives.) Transfer the mixture to a bowl.

4. Add the buttermilk and stir with a spoon until the dough comes together into a shaggy mass. Do not overmix.

CONTINUED

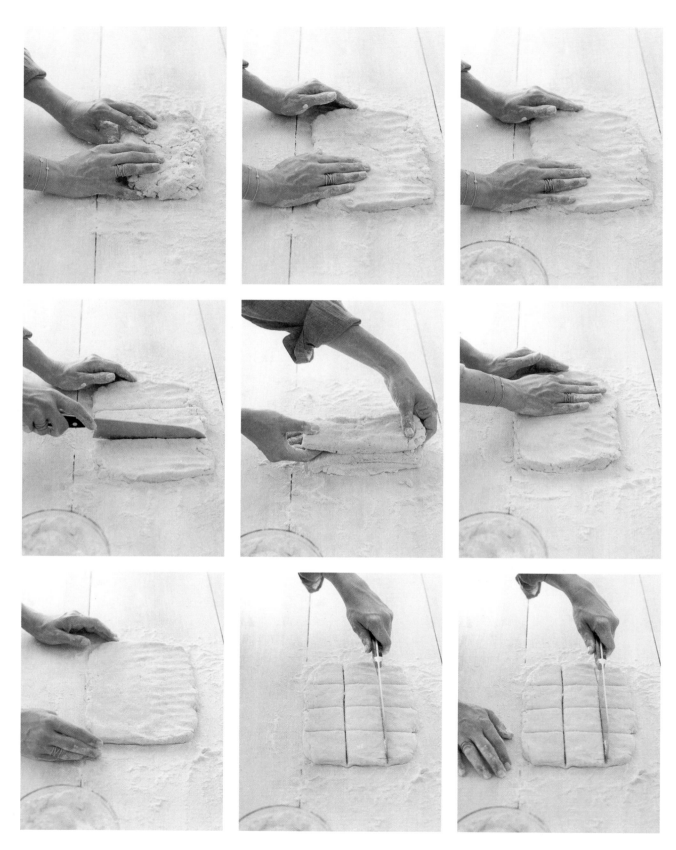

5. Turn the dough out onto a lightly floured work surface. Dust the top of the dough with a bit more flour and bring together gently into a loose ball. Pat the dough into a rectangle about ¾ in [2 cm] thick.

6. Using a sharp knife, cut the dough into thirds. Stack the pieces on top of one another and pat out into a rectangle ¾ in [2 cm] thick again, flouring the surface lightly as needed to prevent the dough from sticking.

7. Cut the dough into thirds again. Stack the pieces on top of one another and pat into a rectangle with a final thickness of about ¾ in [2 cm].

8. Dust the blade of a sharp knife with flour and cut the dough into 12 even squares. Transfer the squares to the prepared baking sheet and bake for 13 to 15 minutes, until the biscuits are lightly golden on top and a rich, golden brown on the bottom. The biscuits are best served warm out of the oven (though a few minutes in the oven will revive slightly stale biscuits).

MAKE AHEAD: The biscuits may be frozen before baking. Place the unbaked biscuits on a baking sheet, cover with plastic wrap, and freeze until solid. Remove the firm biscuits from the freezer, place in an airtight bag, and store in the freezer for up to 3 months. Bake the biscuits directly from the freezer, but allow a few extra minutes baking time.

pro tip

Most biscuit recipes direct you to fold the dough into thirds several times to create layers of dough that result in puffy biscuits (similar to the way croissants and puff pastry are made). I think cutting the dough into thirds and stacking the pieces together works even better, because when you fold the dough, the side with the crease doesn't rise as high.

You can use a round biscuit cutter to make the biscuits round but cutting them into squares is much easier (no scraps). And who says biscuits have to be round?

monterey jack & jalapeño cornbread

heads up

This cornbread has a little kick, but it's not what you'd call spicy. That said, if you're cooking for little ones, you might cut back or omit the jalapeño peppers.

CORNBREAD IS A WEEKNIGHT dinner staple at my house. In fact, my kids love it so much that I'm constantly swatting their hands away from the breadbasket so that they don't fill up. Here, I've jazzed up my basic recipe with some jalapeño peppers and jack cheese. I know that baking at dinnertime might seem a little ambitious, but you can make this batter in just 15 minutes. And I always serve cornbread in place of a starch. Serves 6

1¼ cups [155 g] all-purpose flour

¾ cup [105 g] yellow cornmeal

1 Tbsp baking powder

¼ cup sugar

1 tsp salt

2 eggs

2 Tbsp honey

¾ cup [180 ml] milk

2 Tbsp seeded and minced jalapeño pepper, from 2 jalapeños

½ cup (1 stick) [110 g] unsalted butter, melted, plus more for serving

⅔ cup [70 g] grated Monterey jack or Cheddar cheese

pro tip

Be careful when cooking with jalapeño peppers. The juices can burn. Wear gloves or wash your hands immediately after handling jalapeños. And, whatever you do, don't touch your eyes.

1. Preheat the oven to 350°F [180°C] and set an oven rack in the middle position. Butter and flour an 8-in [20-cm] square glass or metal baking pan. (Alternatively, use a nonstick cooking spray with flour in it, such as Baker's Joy or Pam Baking Spray with Flour.)

2. In a large bowl, whisk together the flour, cornmeal, baking powder, sugar, and salt. Set aside.

3. In a medium bowl, break up the eggs with a whisk. Whisk in the honey, followed by the milk and jalapeño. Add the liquid mixture to the dry ingredients, along with the melted butter and cheese. Whisk until just blended.

4. Spoon the batter into the prepared pan and smooth the top with a spatula. Bake for about 30 minutes, until the top is lightly golden in the center and golden brown around the edges. Let the cornbread cool for a few minutes on a wire rack, then cut into squares right from the pan. Serve warm with butter.

5. Cornbread tastes best when served right out of the oven, but leftovers can be stored in an airtight container at room temperature for up to

2 days. To reheat, wrap cornbread in aluminum foil and place in a preheated 350°F [180°C] oven until warm, 10 to 15 minutes.

mini savory cheddar dijon scones

THESE SAVORY SCONES are not only wonderful with soup, they also make darling hors d'oeuvres with wine and cocktails. Feel free to swap out the Cheddar for Gruyère or add some finely chopped fresh herbs along with the chives. You really can't go wrong: the main thing is to serve the scones warm from the oven, when they are at their tender best. Makes 12 small scones

sourcing savvy

If you don't have cake flour, you can substitute 1¾ cups [220 g] all-purpose flour plus ¼ cup [30 g] cornstarch.

1 egg

¾ cup [180 ml] heavy cream

2 Tbsp Dijon mustard

2 cups [230 g] cake flour, plus more for dusting

1 Tbsp baking powder

2 tsp sugar

¾ tsp salt

¼ tsp freshly ground black pepper

5 Tbsp [70 g] cold unsalted butter, cut into ½-in [12-mm] pieces, plus more at room temperature for serving

1 cup [115 g] diced or shredded sharp Cheddar cheese

2 Tbsp finely chopped fresh chives

1 egg, beaten, for brushing

1. Preheat the oven to 400°F [200°C] and set an oven rack in the middle position. Line a 13-by-18-in [33-by-46-cm] baking sheet with parchment paper.

2. In a small bowl, whisk together the egg, heavy cream, and mustard. Set aside.

3. In a large bowl, whisk together the cake flour, baking powder, sugar, salt, and pepper. Add the pieces of cold butter; use your fingertips to rub the butter into the dry ingredients until the mixture resembles course crumbs with some pea-size clumps of butter. Stir in the cheese and chives.

4. Add the cream mixture and use a rubber spatula to mix until the dough comes together into a cohesive mass. It will be a little sticky.

5. Lightly dust a work surface with all-purpose flour, then place the scone dough on the surface. Dust the dough very lightly with flour and knead gently a few times until the dough comes together into a ball. (Sprinkle more flour, little by little, if the dough is too sticky to work with.) Divide the dough in half and pat each half into a 5-in [12-cm] round, then cut each round into 6 wedges. Transfer the wedges to the prepared baking sheet, spacing them about 1 in [2.5 cm] apart. Brush with the beaten

egg, then bake for 10 to 12 minutes, until the tops are lightly golden and firm to the touch. Serve warm out of the oven with butter. Scones are best served fresh out of the oven or on the same day.

MAKE AHEAD: The dough can be made, shaped, and refrigerated overnight, and then baked directly from the fridge as directed. Or, to freeze the dough, place the raw scones on a baking sheet, cover with plastic wrap, and put them in the freezer until they are solid. Transfer them to an airtight container and freeze for up to 3 months. To bake, remove the scones from the freezer while you preheat the oven. Cook as directed, but allow a few extra minutes baking time.

garlic & herb ciabatta

THERE IS ALWAYS HAPPINESS *chez moi* when garlic bread is on the menu, so this easy recipe is in the regular rotation. I use a store-bought Italian ciabatta (pronounced *cha-bah-tah*) because it has a crisp crust and soft, porous texture ideal for soaking up indecent amounts of garlic butter. To mellow the raw garlic flavor, I cook the garlic butter on the stovetop before spooning it onto the bread. Garlic bread should pack a punch, but it shouldn't knock you out! Serves 4 to 6

2 Tbsp extra-virgin olive oil

6 Tbsp [85 g] unsalted butter

3 garlic cloves, minced

½ tsp salt

¼ tsp freshly ground black pepper

2 Tbsp finely chopped fresh Italian parsley

One 1-lb [455-g] loaf ciabatta bread

1. Preheat the oven to 400°F [200°C] and set an oven rack in the middle position.

2. In a small skillet, heat the oil and butter over low heat. When the butter is melted, add the garlic and cook, stirring occasionally, until softened and fragrant but not browned, 1 to 2 minutes. Off the heat, stir in the salt, pepper, and parsley.

3. Slice the ciabatta in half horizontally. Brush or spoon the garlic butter mixture over the cut sides of the bread, covering completely. Place the halves back together again and wrap in aluminum foil. Place directly on the oven rack and bake until warm, about 10 minutes. Unwrap the bread and place it back in the oven for about 5 minutes, or until toasted and crisp. Cut into slices and serve.

why it's important to follow a few firm rules

It is often said that cooking is an art and baking is a science. For instance, in cooking, you create a dish as you would a painting—tasting and adjusting the flavor as you go and adding your own personal style. In baking, however, you follow certain formulas and stick to the script; otherwise your cakes may fall, your cookies may spread, your piecrusts may be tough, and so on. But I don't want to scare you away from baking! You can easily prevent baking disasters by understanding the basics, avoiding substitutions, and following a few simple rules.

MEASURE PROPERLY

This is the most important rule in baking. Ideally, you should weigh your ingredients on a digital scale but if you don't have one, the proper way to measure dry ingredients is using the "spoon and level" method: spoon the ingredients into a dry measuring cup and level or "sweep" the top with a straight edge. This might seem nitpicky, but it's important. A cup of flour measured in volume can vary by several ounces, so if you scoop it into the measuring cup and pack it in, you'll end up with way too much flour and your baked goods will be dry. The only ingredient that you should ever pack into a cup is brown sugar.

Liquid ingredients should always be measured in clear measuring cups with pour spouts and gradations on the side of the cup. I love the ones that allow you to see the measurement marks from overhead.

INVEST IN A GOOD MIXER

I have a 5-qt [5-L] KitchenAid mixer that I leave on the countertop and use for just about everything. If you buy a good one, it will last for decades—mine once fell on the floor and it still works! An electric hand mixer is a good alternative.

USE ROOM-TEMPERATURE INGREDIENTS

When a recipe calls for room-temperature ingredients, it's important to comply. Cold butter cannot be creamed, and cold eggs can shock and curdle a batter. It's best to leave ingredients on the countertop overnight, but I confess that I almost never remember to do this. To quickly bring eggs to room temperature, place them in a bowl and run them under warm tap water for a few minutes. You can soften butter in the microwave, but keep a close eye on it because if it gets too soft, it can ruin a recipe. I usually cut the sticks into 1-in [2.5-cm] pieces and zap them at 50 percent power in 10-second intervals until just softened.

CHECK YOUR OVEN TEMPERATURE

It's a good idea to check your oven temperature every so often to be sure it's accurate. Along the same lines, when you're baking, try not to open your oven to peek until the recommended cook time is up. Otherwise, you'll let cool air in, which interrupts the baking process. The only exception to this rule is to rotate pans halfway through baking if you're cooking with multiple pans or if your oven has a hot spot; just do it quickly so you don't cool the oven down.

DON'T MAKE SUBSTITUTIONS

Baking is chemistry and, unfortunately, there are no good substitutes for all-purpose flour, sugar, butter, or eggs. However, the "recipe police" won't come after you if you change little things that don't alter the chemistry of the recipe, like adding nuts or swapping orange zest for lemon zest.

USE A LIGHT HAND

If you've spent any time baking, you've likely come across the phrase "do not overmix." This is because once you add flour to a recipe, mixing encourages gluten development, which creates a chewy or tough texture. We knead bread dough to activate gluten so that the bread is nice and chewy—but we don't want that in tender cakes and muffins. So, when a recipe says, "do not overmix," stir only until the batter is uniform. Similarly, for scones and biscuits, recipes usually instruct, "Do not overwork the dough." Again, you don't want to activate the gluten, and you also don't want to soften or warm the butter—the cold chunks of butter steam in the oven, lifting the dough to make tender and flaky baked goods.

UNDERSTAND LEAVENING AGENTS

Baking powder and baking soda are used in many recipes to make baked goods rise without the need for yeast. They are not interchangeable. Baking soda needs acidic ingredients to activate, so it is used in recipes that contain buttermilk, brown sugar, lemon juice, cocoa powder, etc. Baking powder, on the other hand, needs only liquid to activate, so it is used in recipes that do not contain acidic ingredients. Some recipes, like chocolate chip cookies, call for both baking powder and baking soda. These recipes typically contain some sort of acidic ingredient, but baking soda alone is not enough to lift the volume of batter in the recipe, so baking powder is added to pick up the slack.

ADD INGREDIENTS IN LITTLE PILES

Maybe it's just me, but I often lose track of what I'm doing in the kitchen. I always add ingredients to the bowl in neat little piles when I'm baking so that I can see clearly what I've already added.

LINE PANS PROPERLY

Parchment paper is ideal for lining cookie and cake pans, and provides easy removal and cleanup. Plus, it can be reused again and again. You can also use professional-style silicone mats; they are more durable than parchment and can be used forever. For bar cookies, make removal easier by lining the pans with heavy-duty aluminum foil coated with cooking spray.

Just lift the block out onto a board and cut. Be sure to use good-quality foil, such as Reynolds Wrap Heavy Duty; inexpensive or uncommon brands can stick.

PREPARE BAKING PANS PROPERLY

I usually use nonstick spray or nonstick spray with flour for quick, effective coverage. Hold the pan over the sink or open dishwasher when spraying to avoid a mess.

MEASURE AND SCOOP BATTER EVENLY

Use cookie scoops and ice cream scoops with triggers for measuring cookie dough, muffins, and cupcakes. The scoops will be more consistent, the baked goods will cook more evenly, and it's a faster way to get the job done.

desserts

I have loved to bake ever since I was a little girl. In fact, one of my clearest childhood memories is baking my grandmother's famous spiced pumpkin bread with my mom in the '70s-style kitchen of our old house. We brought that bread to every neighborhood potluck and holiday party. Now the recipe lives on my blog, and I think my grandmother would be thrilled to know that it's become one of the most popular pumpkin bread recipes on the Internet!

Much as I love making desserts, I know that many people think of themselves as people who "don't bake." Even if they happily don an apron to make dinner every night, when it comes to dessert, they head straight for the nearest bakery. They might think, "Baking is too fussy; I'm not the measuring type," or perhaps they aren't comfortable with the blind faith that baking requires. In cooking, you can taste and watch the food as you go. But in baking, you create a batter or dough and then rely on a mysterious chemical reaction to happen in the oven, crossing your fingers that everything turns out right.

If you're a reluctant baker, read the baking tips on pages 238–239. Then, start with something simple, like the Toffee Almond Sandies (page 253) or No-Churn Cheesecake Ice Cream (page 242). Once you have success with those, move on to the Chocolate Croissant Bread Pudding (page 257) or Red, White & Blue Summer Berry Trifle (page 244), which are slightly more involved but no more difficult. From there, you can tackle pies, cakes, and cupcakes—even homemade candy. The reality is that baking is not hard. As long as you start with a good recipe and follow it to a "T," you'll have success.

no-churn cheesecake ice cream with graham cracker–pecan crumble

MICHAEL LOVES CHEESECAKE—IN FACT, it was his mother's bribe of choice his entire childhood—so when he tried this ice cream for the first time, his eyes practically rolled back in his head. It's rich and slightly tangy, with a spot-on cheesecake flavor. You'll be glad to know that the recipe does not require an ice cream machine. Simply blitz all of the ingredients in a food processor and put the mixture in the freezer. Like magic, it freezes up smooth and creamy. Makes about 4 cups [960 ml]

FOR THE CHEESECAKE ICE CREAM

1 cup [240 ml] heavy cream

8 oz [230 g] cream cheese

½ cup [120 ml] sour cream

1 cup [200 g] granulated sugar

½ tsp lemon zest, from 1 lemon

2 Tbsp fresh lemon juice

Pinch of salt

FOR THE GRAHAM CRACKER-PECAN CRUMBLE

8 whole graham crackers [125 g], broken into pieces

⅓ cup [40 g] pecans

3 Tbsp packed dark brown sugar

4 Tbsp [55 g] unsalted butter, melted

Pinch of salt

1. To make the ice cream: In a food processor fitted with the steel blade, combine all of the ingredients. Blend until smooth and creamy, and the sugar is completely dissolved, 2 to 3 minutes. Transfer to a plastic container or loaf pan; cover and freeze until solid, about 8 hours or overnight.

2. To make the crumble: Preheat the oven to 325°F [170°C] and set an oven rack in the middle position. Line a rimmed 13-by-18-in [33-by-46-cm] baking sheet with parchment paper.

3. In a food processor fitted with the steel blade, combine the graham crackers, pecans, brown sugar, butter, and salt; pulse until finely chopped. It's okay to leave some small chunks; just be sure the brown sugar is incorporated. Transfer the mixture to the prepared baking sheet and press into a compact layer about ⅛ in [3 mm] thick, like a crust (don't worry if the edges are uneven). Bake until golden around

the edges, 12 to 15 minutes; let cool to room temperature, then break into chunks. (Or, instead of a making a crumble, you can break the crust into larger shards and serve the pieces as a "cookie" garnish.)

4. Scoop the ice cream into bowls and top with the crumble. The ice cream will keep for a few weeks in the freezer, and the crumble will keep in an airtight container at room temperature for up to a week.

red, white & blue summer berry trifle

heads up

Be sure to plan ahead, as the trifle needs to sit in the fridge at least 8 hours before serving.

BERRY TRIFLES MAKE WONDERFUL (and patriotic) summer party desserts. Not only are they gorgeous, they feed a crowd and can be made in advance. The only drawback is that, with all their layers, they can be time-consuming to make from scratch. I save time by using high-quality store-bought ingredients, like crisp Savoiardi biscuits (a.k.a. crisp ladyfingers), cream cheese, and raspberry jam. The result is a dazzling, delicious trifle that can be made in 30 minutes.

Use a deep, clear glass bowl or a footed glass trifle dish so the pretty layers can be seen. And don't worry if the layers look slightly uneven or if the layers mix a bit—that's the beauty of a trifle. You can also make the trifle in small glasses as individual parfaits. Serves 8 to 10

sourcing savvy

Savoiardi biscuits are crisp ladyfingers, usually sold in the packaged cookie section of the supermarket. Don't confuse them with the soft-sponge cakelike ladyfingers from the bakery—those aren't nearly as good.

1½ lb [680 g] strawberries, hulled and cut into ¼-in [6-mm] slices

¾ lb [340 g] raspberries

¾ lb [340 g] blueberries

¾ cup [225 g] seedless raspberry jam, best quality

1½ cups [360 ml] cold heavy whipping cream

16 oz [455 g] cream cheese, at room temperature

1¾ cups [200 g] confectioners' sugar

1 tsp vanilla extract

One 7-oz [200-g] package crisp ladyfingers (also called Savoiardi biscuits)

Fresh mint, for garnish (optional)

CONTINUED

Folding is a technique used to mix a light and airy ingredient, like whipped cream, into a heavier mixture, like sweetened cream cheese, without deflating the lighter mixture. To fold, place the heavier mixture in a bowl and top with the lighter mixture. Use a spatula to cut through the middle of the two mixtures down to the bottom of the bowl. Pull the spatula toward you, scooping up some of the heavier mixture. In one sweeping motion, fold the scooped up portion of the heavier mixture over the lighter mixture. Turn the bowl a quarter turn and repeat the motions, scraping the sides of the bowl occasionally, until the ingredients are well combined.

1. Set aside a few of each berry for topping your finished trifle.

2. In a large bowl, heat the raspberry jam in the microwave for about 1 minute, or until hot and liquidy. Add the fresh berries and toss to coat. Let sit while you prepare the rest of the recipe, stirring occasionally.

3. In the bowl of an electric mixer fitted with the whisk attachment (or beaters), whip the heavy cream until stiff peaks form. Set aside.

4. In another large bowl, use an electric mixer fitted with the paddle attachment (or beaters) to beat the cream cheese with the confectioners' sugar until smooth and creamy. Beat in the vanilla, then beat in a third of the whipped cream. Using a large rubber spatula, fold in the rest of the whipped cream until well combined (see Pro Tip).

5. Use a 9-in [23-cm] round trifle dish or glass bowl with a 14-cup [3.3-L] capacity. Line the bottom of the dish with a layer of ladyfingers, breaking into pieces as necessary. Follow with one-third of the berry-jam mixture (including one-third of the juices), then one-third of the cream cheese mixture. Add another layer of ladyfingers, berries, and cream, and then a third, ending with the cream; for the last layer of cream, leave a 1-in [2.5-cm] border around the edge showing the fruit beneath. Garnish with the reserved whole berries and mint (if using). Refrigerate for at least 8 hours or overnight before serving.

persian lime "key lime" pie

I USE PERSIAN LIMES (otherwise known as ordinary supermarket limes) to make my "Key lime" pie. Unless you live in the Florida Keys, key limes are near impossible to find. And furthermore, they're so tiny that you'd need to juice at least twenty of them for this recipe. No thank you! Persian limes make an exceptional Key lime pie, and are a much better alternative to bracingly tart bottled Key lime juice. I think this pie tastes every bit as authentic as the real deal—plus it's easier to make. Serves 8 to 10

FOR THE CRUST

1½ cups [190 g] finely crushed graham cracker crumbs, from about 12 whole graham crackers

⅓ cup [70 g] packed light brown sugar

4 Tbsp [55 g] unsalted butter, melted

FOR THE FILLING

Two 14-oz [400-g] cans sweetened condensed milk

1 cup [240 g] plain Greek yogurt (2 percent or whole milk)

1 Tbsp grated lime zest

¾ cup [180 ml] fresh lime juice

FOR THE TOPPING

1 cup [240 ml] cold heavy whipping cream

2 Tbsp confectioners' sugar

1 tsp grated lime zest

10 thin lime slices

heads up

With no eggs, it's almost hard to believe that this pie will set, but have faith—it will. And be sure to zest the limes before you squeeze the juice from them, as it's near impossible to do afterward. You'll need 8 to 10 limes total for this recipe.

sourcing savvy

Sweetened condensed milk is canned milk from which water has been removed, and sugar has been added. Be sure not to confuse it with evaporated milk, which is usually sold right alongside.

pro tip

Confectioners' sugar contains a small amount of cornstarch. The cornstarch helps stabilize whipped cream, keeping it perky. It's important to add the sugar after the peaks have begun to form in the cream, otherwise the cornstarch won't have the intended effect.

1. To make the crust: Preheat the oven to 375°F [190°C] and set an oven rack in the middle position.

2. In a medium bowl, combine the graham cracker crumbs, brown sugar, and melted butter; stir with a fork first, and then your hands until the mixture is well combined. Using your fingers and the bottom of a clean glass, press the crumbs firmly into the bottom and up the sides of a 9-by-1.5-in [23-by-4-cm] pie pan. The crust should be about ¼ in [6 mm] thick.

3. Bake for 10 minutes, until just slightly browned. Let the crust cool on a wire rack.

CONTINUED

4. To make the filling: Lower the oven temperature to 350°F [180°C].

5. In a large bowl, whisk together the sweetened condensed milk, yogurt, lime zest, and lime juice. Pour the thick mixture into the cooked graham cracker crust. Bake for 15 minutes. Let cool at room temperature for 30 minutes, then place in the refrigerator to chill thoroughly, about 3 hours.

6. To make the topping: In the bowl of an electric mixer fitted with the whisk attachment (or beaters), beat the heavy cream until soft peaks form. Add the confectioners' sugar and beat until stiff peaks form. (Alternatively, the whipped cream can be beaten by hand with a whisk.) Top the pie with whipped cream and sprinkle with lime zest. Decorate with lime slices.

MAKE AHEAD: You can make the crust a day ahead of time, but the filling should be added on the day of serving; otherwise the crust will get soggy.

old-fashioned ginger spice cookies

heads up

Allow a few hours for the dough to chill in the fridge before baking.

EVERY YEAR, MY DAUGHTER AND I bake these cookies for her holiday bake sale and every year, they sell like hotcakes. Soft and chewy with a crackled sugar crust, they have just the right balance of spices to please kids and adults alike. You'll note that the recipe calls for black pepper. I promise, no one will know it's there, but it adds a delightful little kick that lingers on the palate. Makes 38 cookies

2⅓ cups [290 g] all-purpose flour

2 tsp baking soda

¼ tsp salt

2 tsp ground ginger

1 tsp ground cinnamon

½ tsp ground allspice

¼ tsp ground cloves

⅛ tsp freshly ground black pepper

¾ cup (1½ sticks) [165 g] unsalted butter, at room temperature

¼ cup plus 2 Tbsp [75 g] granulated sugar

¼ cup plus 2 Tbsp [80 g] packed light brown sugar

1 egg

⅓ cup [115 g] molasses

½ cup [100 g] raw sugar (also called turbinado or demerara sugar), for rolling cookies

1. In a medium bowl, whisk together the flour, baking soda, salt, ginger, cinnamon, allspice, cloves, and black pepper.

2. In the bowl of an electric mixer fitted with the paddle attachment (or beaters), beat the butter and the granulated and light brown sugars until light and fluffy, about 2 minutes. Beat in the egg and molasses. Add the flour mixture and mix until combined. Chill the dough in the refrigerator until firm, a few hours.

3. Meanwhile, preheat the oven to 350°F [180°C] and set two racks in the centermost positions. Line two 13-by-18-in [33-by-46-cm] baking sheets with parchment paper.

4. Form tablespoons of dough into balls and roll in the raw sugar to coat generously. Arrange the dough balls about 2½ in [6 cm] apart on the prepared baking sheets. Bake for 9 to 10 minutes, rotating the sheets from top to bottom and front to back midway through, until puffed and set. Let cool on the baking sheets for a few minutes, then transfer to a wire rack to cool completely. Store in an airtight container at room temperature for up to 3 days.

toffee almond sandies

THIS RECIPE WAS SENT TO ME by Kelly Pittman, along with hundreds of others, for a holiday cookie contest I ran on my blog many years ago. The cookies not only won my contest, they also became a much-loved Segal family favorite. While the cookies may look plain, when you bite into them, you discover a buttery, sweet shortbread studded with melted toffee bits and crunchy almonds. They're wonderfully good, easy to make, and long lasting. In other words, the perfect holiday cookie. Makes 9 dozen cookies

heads up

This recipe makes a ton! It's ideal for a bake sale or gift-giving but if you'd like to make less, the recipe can easily be halved.

3½ cups [440 g] all-purpose flour

1 cup [125 g] whole-wheat flour

1 tsp baking soda

1 tsp cream of tartar

1 tsp salt

1 cup (2 sticks) [220 g] unsalted butter, at room temperature

1 cup [200 g] granulated sugar, plus more for rolling the cookies

1 cup [115 g] confectioners' sugar

1 cup [240 ml] vegetable oil

2 eggs

1 tsp almond extract

2 cups [240 g] chopped slivered almonds

1 heaping cup [170 g] English toffee bits

1. Preheat the oven to 350°F [180°C] and set two racks in the center-most positions. Line two 13-by-18-in [33-by-46-cm] baking sheets with parchment paper.

2. In a medium bowl, combine the all-purpose flour, whole-wheat flour, baking soda, cream of tartar, and salt; mix well.

3. In the bowl of an electric mixer fitted with the paddle attachment (or beaters), cream the butter, granulated sugar, and confectioners' sugar until well combined, 1 to 2 minutes. Scrape down the sides of the bowl with a spatula, then beat in the oil, eggs, and almond extract. Add the dry ingredients to the bowl and mix on low speed until combined. Mix in the almonds and toffee bits.

4. Shape the dough into 1-in [2.5-cm] balls and roll in sugar. Place the balls about 2 in [5 cm] apart on the prepared baking sheets and flatten with a fork. Bake, rotating the sheets halfway through, for 14 to 17 minutes, or until lightly browned. Let the cookies cool on the baking sheets for a few minutes, and then transfer to a wire rack to cool completely. Store the cookies in an airtight container for up to 1 week.

apple-oat-pecan crisp

THIS RUSTIC DESSERT OF tart apples bubbling away under a crisp and buttery streusel is a longtime favorite of mine. In fact, it's one of the very first recipes I posted on my blog nearly ten years ago. It's wonderful served warm out of the oven with a scoop of vanilla ice cream—though, truthfully, I like the cold leftovers with my morning coffee just as much. Serves 6

¼ cup plus 2 Tbsp [50 g] all-purpose flour

¼ cup plus 2 Tbsp [80 g] packed light brown sugar

¼ cup plus 6 Tbsp [130 g] granulated sugar

Pinch of salt

6 Tbsp [85 g] very cold unsalted butter, cut into ½-in [12-mm] pieces

1 cup [115 g] pecans, chopped

½ cup [50 g] old-fashioned rolled oats (not quick or instant)

2½ lb [1.1 kg] tart baking apples (about 5 large), peeled, cored, and cut into slices about ¼ in [6 mm] thick

Vanilla ice cream, for serving

1. Preheat the oven to 350°F [180°C] and set an oven rack in the middle position.

2. In a food processor fitted with the steel blade, pulse the flour, brown sugar, ¼ cup [50 g] of the granulated sugar, and the salt until combined. Add the butter and pulse until the mixture resembles coarse meal. (Alternatively, the flour, sugar, and salt mixture can be mixed by hand, and the butter can be "cut in" with a pastry cutter, two knives, or your fingers.) Transfer the mixture to a medium bowl and stir in the pecans and oats. Set aside.

3. Generously butter a shallow 2-qt [2-L] baking dish. In a medium bowl, toss the apples with the remaining 6 tablespoons [80 g] granulated sugar. Transfer the apple mixture to the prepared baking dish and cover with the pecan-oat mixture. Bake for 40 to 50 minutes, or until the apples are tender when pierced and the topping is toasted. Serve warm with vanilla ice cream, if desired.

chocolate croissant
bread pudding

GIVEN ITS ORIGIN AS A way to use up stale bread, bread pudding is usually thought of as a thrifty, humble dessert. But this recipe for flaky croissants baked in bourbon-spiked custard with pockets of melted chocolate is decadent in every way. And yet it's almost absurdly easy to make: you simply whisk the custard, pour it over the croissants and chocolate, let soak, and bake.

Though there's bourbon in the recipe, the bread pudding does not have a boozy flavor. I recommend it for depth of flavor, but for those who avoid alcohol, it's fine to replace the bourbon with coffee or more half-and-half. Serves 10 to 12

heads up

The bread pudding needs to chill for at least 1 hour or overnight before baking, so plan accordingly.

¾ lb [340 g] croissants, torn into 1-in [2.5-cm] chunks

4 oz [115 g] semisweet chocolate, chopped into small pieces

5 eggs

3 cups [720 ml] half-and-half

1 cup [200 g] sugar

1 tsp vanilla extract

¼ tsp salt

¼ cup [60 ml] bourbon

Vanilla ice cream, for serving (optional)

sourcing savvy

When a recipe calls for chopped semisweet chocolate, it can be tempting to save time and substitute chocolate chips. However, chocolate chips and chocolate are not always interchangeable in recipes. Chocolate chips are made to hold their shape when hot and to harden when cooled—a plus for chocolate chip cookies, but not always for other desserts.

1. Generously butter a 9-by-13-in [23-by-33-cm] baking dish. Place the torn croissants in the dish. Scatter the chopped chocolate over the top and toss gently with your hands to mix.

2. In a large bowl, whisk the eggs until lightly beaten. Add the half-and-half, sugar, vanilla, salt, and bourbon; whisk until well combined.

3. Pour the custard evenly over the croissants and chocolate. Cover and refrigerate for at least 1 hour or up to 24 hours to allow the croissants to soak up the custard.

4. Preheat the oven to 350°F [180°C] and set an oven rack in the middle position.

5. Cover the dish with aluminum foil and bake for 25 minutes. Remove the foil and continue baking until the top is golden and the center is set, about 20 minutes more. Spoon into bowls and top with vanilla ice cream, if desired.

chocolate buttercrunch with sea salt

I MAKE BATCHES AND BATCHES of this crunchy toffee and chocolate candy over the holidays. It's perfect for gift giving, easy to whip up with very few ingredients, and crazy-addictive! The crunchy toffee layer is made by heating a sugar and butter syrup until it reaches 300° to 310°F [150° to 154°C], the "hard-crack" stage. I highly recommend using a foolproof candy thermometer for this process, but you can also test the syrup the old-fashioned way. When the syrup starts to darken, use a teaspoon to drop a dollop into ice-cold water. It should harden immediately so that you can snap it in two. If it bends, it's not quite ready. Makes about 25 pieces

2 cups [230 g] roughly chopped pecans

1 cup (2 sticks) [220 g] unsalted butter

1½ cups [300 g] sugar

1 Tbsp light corn syrup

1 cup [175 g] semisweet chocolate or chocolate chips, best quality, such as Ghirardelli or Guittard

½ tsp flaky sea salt or kosher salt

pro tips

There are several different styles of candy thermometers. I prefer the clip-on rectangular model with the thermometer encased in the frame (pictured on page 17). With this design, the thermometer bulb does not touch the bottom of the pan (which would affect the reading), even if you rest the thermometer in the pan.

Toffee hardens quickly, making the pan difficult to clean. To loosen the toffee, add water to the pan and bring it to a boil.

1. Preheat the oven to 350°F [180°C] and set an oven rack in the middle position. Line a 9-by-13-in [23-by-33-cm] metal baking pan with parchment paper so that it goes up the sides of the pan. (Place a few dabs of softened butter on the pan to secure the parchment, if necessary.)

2. Spread the pecans in a single layer in the prepared pan. Bake until fragrant, about 8 minutes; let cool in the pan.

3. Remove half of the pecans from the pan and set aside in a bowl. Spread the remaining nuts evenly around the pan.

4. In a medium saucepan, melt the butter over medium heat. Add the sugar, corn syrup, and 3 tablespoons [45 ml] water and stir well to combine; bring the mixture to a boil. Continue boiling gently over medium heat, without stirring, until the mixture turns a caramel color and reaches 300°F [150°C] on an instant-read or candy thermometer, 10 to 12 minutes.

5. When the syrup is ready, pour it evenly over the nuts in the pan. Wait for the syrup to solidify, 4 to 5 minutes, then immediately scatter the

chocolate over the top. Wait for the chocolate to soften, about 3 minutes, and then use an offset spatula or the back of a spoon to smear the chocolate into an even layer. Sprinkle the salt over the top, followed by the reserved nuts.

6. Place the baking sheet in the freezer for 30 to 35 minutes, or until just set (no longer or it won't break into chunks easily). Use the parchment overhang to lift the buttercrunch slab out of the pan, then use your hands to break it into uneven pieces. Store the candy in an airtight container for 2 weeks in the refrigerator or at room temperature.

indoor s'mores

THESE BARS TASTE JUST LIKE the campfire classic, only taken up a notch with a graham cracker crust, chocolate ganache filling, and silky meringue topping. Kids *love* them! The only time-consuming part of the recipe is waiting for each layer to set before proceeding with the next. I use the freezer to speed this process along.

Just like real s'mores, these bars are wonderfully gooey. I serve them on dessert plates with forks or in cupcake liners with lots of napkins. Makes 16 to 25 squares, depending on how large you cut them

sourcing savvy

For the most authentic s'mores taste, use Hershey Bars for the milk chocolate. I use five Hershey's Milk Chocolate Bars (which is just shy of 8 oz [230 g]) and a 4-oz [115-g] Ghirardelli bittersweet baking bar for the chocolate ganache filling.

FOR THE CRUST

2 cups [250 g] graham cracker crumbs, from about 16 whole graham crackers

1½ Tbsp packed light brown sugar

¼ tsp salt

½ cup (1 stick) [110 g] unsalted butter, melted

FOR THE CHOCOLATE GANACHE FILLING

¾ cup [180 ml] heavy cream

4 oz [115 g] bittersweet chocolate, chopped

8 oz [230 g] milk chocolate, chopped

FOR THE MARSHMALLOW MERINGUE TOPPING

3 egg whites

¾ cup [150 g] granulated sugar

½ tsp vanilla extract

¼ tsp cream of tartar

1. To make the crust: Preheat the oven to 350°F [180°C] and set an oven rack in the middle position. Line a 9-in [23-cm] square baking pan with heavy-duty aluminum foil, allowing 2 in [5 cm] of overhang on all sides. Spray with nonstick cooking spray.

2. In a medium bowl, using a fork, mix the graham cracker crumbs, brown sugar, and salt. Add the melted butter and mix until the crumbs are evenly moistened. Press the crumbs evenly and firmly into the bottom of the prepared pan. Bake for 10 minutes. Let cool until set, about 15 minutes.

CONTINUED

3. To make the filling: In a medium microwave-safe bowl, microwave the cream on high for 1 to 2 minutes, or until boiling. Add the bittersweet and milk chocolates and whisk until smooth. If the chocolate doesn't melt completely, place the bowl back in the microwave for 20 seconds and whisk again. (Alternatively, bring the cream to a boil in a small saucepan on the stovetop; then take the pan off the heat and whisk in the chocolates.)

4. Pour the warm chocolate filling evenly over the cooled crust. Use an offset spatula or the back of a spoon to spread the mixture to the edges. Place in the freezer until the chocolate is set, about 45 minutes.

5. To make the topping: Preheat the broiler and set an oven rack about 8 in [20 cm] beneath the heating element.

6. Set a heatproof medium bowl over a saucepan of simmering water (the bottom of the bowl should not touch the water). Add the egg whites and granulated sugar and whisk until the whites are warm and foamy and the sugar is completely dissolved, about 3 minutes. (Rub a little of the mixture between your fingers to make sure you don't feel any grains of sugar.)

7. Transfer the egg white mixture to the bowl of a stand mixer fitted with the whisk (or beaters). Add the vanilla and cream of tartar and beat at medium-high speed (or high speed if using an electric hand mixer) until stiff and glossy, 7 to 8 minutes. You'll know it's ready when you pull the whisk out of the bowl and the meringue peaks and droops over.

8. Mound the meringue on top of the cold chocolate filling, swirling it decoratively. Place the pan in the oven and broil until the meringue is lightly toasted and browned at the tips, 1 to 2 minutes. Keep a close eye on it so it doesn't burn. Place the bars in the freezer until completely cool, about 20 minutes.

9. Using the foil overhang, lift the bars out of the pan and onto a cutting board. Cut into bars, running the knife under hot water and wiping clean between slices. Serve smaller squares in cupcake liners with napkins, and larger squares on small dessert plates with forks. Store leftover bars in an airtight container in the refrigerator, leaving a little space between them so they don't stick, for up to 3 days.

MAKE AHEAD: These bars can be made up to 2 days ahead of time. After toasting the meringue, cover the unsliced bars with plastic wrap and refrigerate. Wait to slice the bars until ready to serve.

luscious lemon squares

ONE DAY, MY DEAR FRIEND Melissa and I got on the subject of lemon squares. Neither of us had a go-to recipe, so we decided to hit the kitchen and create one of our own. Well, we must have made at least 200 lemon squares. After testing every possible variation, we came up with this be-all and end-all recipe. The squares have a crisp short-bread crust and luscious lemon filling. They're not too tart and not too sweet—they're just right. Makes sixteen 2-in [5-cm] squares

FOR THE CRUST

¾ cup [95 g] all-purpose flour

½ cup [60 g] confectioners' sugar, plus more to dust the finished bars

¼ cup [30 g] cornstarch

½ tsp salt

½ cup (1 stick) [110 g] cold unsalted butter, cut into ½-in [12-mm] pieces

FOR THE LEMON FILLING

3 eggs

1½ cups [300 g] granulated sugar

5 Tbsp [75 ml] fresh lemon juice, from 2 lemons

1 Tbsp lemon zest

3 Tbsp [25 g] all-purpose flour

1. To make the crust: Preheat the oven to 350°F [180°C] and set an oven rack in the middle position.

2. Cover a 9-in [23-cm] square baking pan with heavy-duty aluminum foil, allowing 2 in [5 cm] of overhang on all sides to help removal from the pan. Spray the foiled pan with nonstick cooking spray.

3. In the bowl of a food processor fitted with the steel blade, combine the flour, confectioners' sugar, cornstarch, and salt. Mix for a few seconds to combine. Add the butter and pulse until the mixture resembles coarse meal, about 10 seconds. Sprinkle the mixture into the prepared pan and press firmly with your fingers into an even layer, building up a thin ½-in [12-mm] edge around the sides (this keeps the filling from spilling beneath the crust). Refrigerate for 30 minutes.

4. Bake the crust until lightly golden, 15 to 20 minutes.

CONTINUED

pro tips

Adding cornstarch to the crust makes it crisp yet tender.

When a recipe calls for both juice and zest be sure to zest the lemon before juicing.

5. While the crust is baking, make the filling: In a medium bowl, whisk together the eggs, granulated sugar, lemon juice and zest, and flour. When the crust comes out of the oven, give the lemon mixture a quick final stir and then pour it over the top of the crust. Immediately return the pan to the oven and bake for another 20 to 25 minutes, or until the topping is set and firm. Let cool on a rack to room temperature, at least 30 minutes, then cover and chill in the refrigerator until cold (the bars are much easier to cut when cold).

6. To cut, use the foil overhang to lift the baked square out of the pan and onto a cutting board. Loosen the foil from the edges of the crust, using a knife if necessary. Using a sharp knife, trim the edges off, then cut into 2-in [5-cm] squares. Use a fine-mesh sieve to dust the squares with confectioners' sugar. Store the finished lemon squares in the refrigerator and serve chilled.

MAKE AHEAD: The bars will keep in an airtight container in the refrigerator for up to 3 days. They also freeze beautifully for up to 1 month. If making ahead, wait until right before serving to cut the bars and dust with confectioners' sugar.

sticky butterscotch banana cake

THIS WARM, COMFORTING CAKE is a fun twist on the classic English dessert, sticky toffee pudding—which is not really pudding at all, but rather a moist cake made with dates covered in a sticky toffee sauce. It's one of the most popular desserts on my website. In fact, one reader wrote to me that she came across the recipe while looking for a bake-off contest cake. Trusting the reviews, she made it without doing a trial run and just entered it into the contest. Much to her delight, she won!
Serves 9 to 12

FOR THE CAKE

1¾ cups [220 g] all-purpose flour

1 tsp baking powder

1 tsp baking soda

¼ tsp salt

½ cup (1 stick) [110 g] unsalted butter, melted and slightly cooled

¾ cup [150 g] granulated sugar

2 eggs

1 cup [240 g] mashed bananas, from 2 to 3 very ripe bananas

2 Tbsp fresh lemon juice, from 1 lemon

1½ tsp vanilla extract

FOR THE BUTTERSCOTCH SAUCE

1¼ [300 ml] cups heavy cream

½ cup [110 g] packed dark brown sugar

½ cup [120 ml] light corn syrup

4 Tbsp [55 g] unsalted butter

Pinch of salt

Sliced perfectly ripe bananas, for serving

Chopped pecans, for serving

1. To make the cake: Preheat the oven to 350°F [180°C] and set an oven rack in the middle position. Butter and flour an 8-in [20-cm] square baking dish. (Alternatively, use a nonstick cooking spray with flour in it, such as Baker's Joy or Pam Baking Spray with Flour.)

2. In a medium bowl, whisk together the flour, baking powder, baking soda, and salt.

CONTINUED

3. In the bowl of an electric mixer fitted with the paddle attachment (or beaters), mix the melted butter and granulated sugar until blended. Add the eggs, mashed bananas, lemon juice, and vanilla and mix well.

4. On low speed, stir in the flour mixture until just incorporated. Do not overmix. Pour the batter into the prepared pan and bake until golden, or until a toothpick or cake tester inserted into the center comes out clean, about 35 minutes. Leave the oven on.

5. Meanwhile, make the sauce: In a small heavy saucepan, bring the heavy cream, brown sugar, corn syrup, butter, and salt to a boil over high heat, whisking until the sugar dissolves. Lower the heat to medium-low and cook at a gentle boil, whisking occasionally, until the sauce is slightly thickened, about 15 minutes. It should be the consistency of maple syrup; it will continue to thicken as it cools. Remove the sauce from the heat and let sit.

6. Spoon ⅓ cup [80 ml] of the butterscotch sauce (you'll use the rest for serving) over the top of the hot baked banana cake. Return the cake to the oven and bake until the sauce is bubbling vigorously, about 6 minutes. Let the cake cool in the pan on a wire rack for at least 30 minutes.

7. Cut the cake into 9 squares or 12 rectangles. Serve slightly warm or at room temperature, topped with more warm butterscotch sauce, sliced bananas, and pecans.

MAKE AHEAD: This cake can be made 1 day ahead of time, covered with foil, and kept at room temperature. The sauce can be made several days ahead and stored in the refrigerator. Rewarm the sauce on the stovetop over medium heat when ready to serve; if it seems too thick, add a little heavy cream to thin it to the desired consistency.

glazed pumpkin pound cake

MY MOST CHERISHED FAMILY RECIPE is a spiced pumpkin bread that my grandmother clipped from a magazine in the 1950s. I've been baking it since I was a little girl, and it's still as wonderful today as it was back then. Because it's sweet enough to be dessert, I've always wanted to reinvent it as a pound cake. But, of course, it's never as simple as just baking the batter in a different pan. After many trials, and a lot of input from my wonderful recipe testers, I finally came up with this pumpkin cake version of my grandmother's pumpkin bread. It has quickly become a new family favorite—perfect for when the occasion calls for cake. Serves 16

FOR THE CAKE

3 cups [375 g] all-purpose flour

¾ tsp salt

¾ tsp baking powder

1½ tsp baking soda

1½ tsp ground nutmeg

1½ tsp ground cinnamon

1 tsp ground cloves

¾ tsp ground ginger

1 cup (2 sticks) [220 g] unsalted butter, at room temperature

3 cups [600 g] granulated sugar

3 eggs

One 15-oz [430-g] can 100 percent pure pumpkin, preferably Libby's

FOR THE GLAZE

1¼ cups [145 g] confectioners' sugar

2 Tbsp milk

1 Tbsp unsalted butter, melted

1. To make the cake: Preheat the oven to 325°F [170°C] and set an oven rack in the middle position.

2. Butter and flour a 12-cup [2.8-L] nonstick Bundt pan, making sure to get into all the crevices. (Alternatively, use a nonstick cooking spray with flour in it, such as Baker's Joy or Pam Baking Spray with Flour.)

3. In a large bowl, whisk together the flour, salt, baking powder, baking soda, nutmeg, cinnamon, cloves, and ginger. Set aside.

CONTINUED

4. In the bowl of an electric mixer fitted with the paddle attachment (or beaters), beat the butter and granulated sugar on medium speed until just blended. It will be a little crumbly. Add the eggs one at a time, beating well after each addition and scraping down the sides of the bowl as necessary. Continue beating on medium speed until very light and creamy, about 3 minutes. Beat in the pumpkin, scraping down the sides as necessary. The mixture will look grainy and curdled at this point—that's okay.

5. Gradually add the flour mixture and mix on low speed until combined. Scrape down the sides and bottom of the bowl and mix again until the batter is evenly combined.

6. Transfer the batter to the prepared pan and smooth the top with a rubber spatula. Bake for 85 to 95 minutes, or until a toothpick or cake tester inserted into the center comes out clean. Let the cake cool in the pan on a wire rack for 10 minutes, then turn out onto the rack to cool completely.

7. When the cake is completely cooled, make the glaze: In a medium bowl, whisk together the confectioners' sugar, milk, and melted butter. The glaze should be the consistency of Elmer's glue. If it seems too thin, add a bit more confectioners' sugar.

8. Transfer the cake to a platter. Using a spoon, drizzle the glaze over the top of the cake, nudging it down the sides with the spoon as you go so that it drips down the indentations on the sides (once it starts to set, which is immediately, you can't go back). Let the glaze set completely before serving. Store in a cake dome or covered with foil at room temperature for up to 4 days.

honey's coconut cupcakes

THEY SAY THAT TRAITS usually skip a generation, but in my case they skipped two. My great-grandmother, who was called "Honey" by everyone who knew her, was a baker and caterer. She baked cakes for the whole city of Buffalo, New York, and was especially well known for her coconut cake. Unfortunately, she left no real recipe when she passed, only scribbled notes on an old index card from my mom's green tin recipe box. Once I became the family baker, I took it upon myself to recreate Honey's famous coconut cake. I could never get it quite as "coconut-y" as the original but, finally, I nailed it. The trick was adding coconut milk and shredded coconut to both the cake and the frosting. Makes 24 cupcakes

FOR THE CUPCAKES

1 cup [240 ml] canned unsweetened coconut milk

2 Tbsp fresh lemon juice, from 1 lemon

2½ cups [315 g] all-purpose flour

¼ cup [30 g] cornstarch

½ tsp salt

½ tsp baking soda

1 cup (2 sticks) [220 g] unsalted butter, at room temperature

2 cups [400 g] granulated sugar

2 tsp vanilla extract

4 eggs, at room temperature

1 cup [85 g] sweetened shredded coconut

FOR THE FROSTING

½ cup (1 stick) [110 g] unsalted butter, at room temperature

3 oz [85 g] cream cheese, at room temperature

4 cups [460 g] confectioners' sugar

½ tsp vanilla extract

1 Tbsp canned unsweetened coconut milk

Pinch of salt

1½ cups [130 g] sweetened shredded coconut, for topping

CONTINUED

1. To make the cupcakes: Preheat the oven to 350°F [180°C] and set an oven rack in the middle position. Line two cupcake pans with paper liners. Lightly spray the top of the pans with a nonstick cooking spray with flour, such as Baker's Joy or Pam Baking Spray with Flour, just in case the cupcake tops stick to the pan (don't worry if the spray gets in the liners).

2. In a small bowl, whisk together the coconut milk and lemon juice. Set aside.

3. In a medium bowl, whisk together the flour, cornstarch, salt, and baking soda. Set aside.

4. In the bowl of an electric mixer fitted with the paddle attachment (or beaters), beat the butter and granulated sugar on medium speed until light and fluffy, about 3 minutes. Beat in the vanilla, then beat in the eggs, one at a time, scraping down the sides of the bowl as necessary.

5. Turn the speed down to low and beat in one-third of the flour mixture, followed by half of the coconut milk–lemon juice mixture. Scrape down the sides of the bowl. Add another one-third of the flour mixture, followed by the remaining coconut milk–lemon juice mixture. Beat in the remaining flour mixture, then scrape down the bowl and beat again until the batter is just combined. Quickly mix in the shredded coconut; do not overmix.

6. Spoon the batter into the prepared cupcake pans, filling each cup about three-fourths full. Bake for 20 to 23 minutes, until the cupcakes are set, lightly golden, and a toothpick or cake tester inserted into the center of a cupcake comes out clean (note that one pan may finish baking before the other). Let cool in the pans for about 10 minutes, then transfer to a wire rack to cool completely.

7. To make the frosting: In the bowl of an electric mixer fitted with the paddle attachment (or beaters), beat the butter and cream cheese until creamy and well combined. Gradually beat in the confectioners' sugar, and then beat in the vanilla, coconut milk, and salt.

8. When the cupcakes are completely cooled, use a butter knife or small offset spatula to swirl the frosting lavishly over the top. Sprinkle with the shredded coconut, pressing it gently so it adheres, and serve.

MAKE AHEAD: The cupcakes can be made and frosted up to 1 day ahead of time. Store in an airtight container at room temperature.

chocolate lover's birthday cake

WHEN MY KIDS WERE BABIES, I started a home-based baking business specializing in special-occasion cakes and cupcakes, mostly for children's birthday parties. Before I opened, I spent weeks testing every vanilla and chocolate cake recipe under the sun, often baking into the wee hours. My husband would wake up in the morning to find the countertops covered with cakes and cupcakes. He thought I'd lost my mind—little did he know I was just discovering my passion for creating great recipes, which was the impetus for starting my blog. Eventually, I created a few recipes that I loved and could rely on. This is the chocolate one. The cake itself is basically a one-bowl recipe. The frosting, modestly adapted from *Cook's Illustrated*, is fast and foolproof—a welcome change from most homemade chocolate frostings, which are temperamental and take hours to cool. This is my son, Zach's, favorite cake. Serves 12 to 14

FOR THE CAKE

2 cups [250 g] all-purpose flour

2 cups [400 g] granulated sugar

1 cup [85 g] natural unsweetened cocoa powder

1 tsp salt

2 tsp baking powder

1 tsp baking soda

2 eggs, lightly beaten

½ cup [120 ml] vegetable oil

1 cup [240 g] sour cream

1 cup [240 ml] boiling water

FOR THE FROSTING

8 oz [230 g] bittersweet or semisweet chocolate, broken into small pieces

1¼ cups (2½ sticks) [275 g] unsalted butter, at cool room temperature

1¼ cups [145 g] confectioners' sugar

½ cup [40 g] natural unsweetened cocoa powder

⅛ tsp salt

¾ cup [180 ml] light corn syrup

1 tsp vanilla extract

1. To make the cake: Preheat the oven to 350°F [180°C] and set a rack in the center position. Lightly butter the bottom of two 9-in [23-cm] round cake pans. Line the bottom of each pan with rounds of parchment paper, and then butter and flour the parchment and the sides of the pans. (Alternatively, use a nonstick cooking spray with flour, such as Baker's Joy or Pam Baking Spray with Flour; keep in mind that you'll still need the parchment paper.)

CONTINUED

2. In the bowl of an electric mixer fitted with the paddle attachment (or beaters), combine the flour, granulated sugar, cocoa powder, salt, baking powder, and baking soda. Mix on low speed for 30 seconds to combine. Add the eggs, oil, and sour cream; mix on low speed until combined, then increase the speed to medium and beat for 2 minutes. Decrease the speed to low and gradually pour in the hot water (be careful to pour very slowly so it doesn't splash). The batter will be soupy. Stop the mixer and scrape down the sides and bottom of the bowl; mix again until evenly combined.

3. Divide the batter evenly between the prepared cake pans. Bake for about 35 minutes, or until a toothpick or cake tester inserted into the center comes out clean. Let the cake layers cool in the pans on a wire rack for 10 minutes. Invert the cakes onto the rack, remove the pans, and cool completely.

4. To make the frosting: Place the chocolate in a microwave-safe bowl and heat in the microwave for 20-second intervals, stirring in between, until it's about three-quarters of the way melted. Stir, allowing the residual heat in the bowl to melt the remaining chocolate completely. If necessary, place the chocolate back in the microwave for a few seconds, but take care not to let the chocolate get too hot (see Pro Tip). Set aside to cool.

5. In a food processor fitted with the steel blade, combine the butter, confectioners' sugar, cocoa powder, and salt and process until smooth, about 30 seconds, scraping down the sides of the bowl as needed. Add the corn syrup and vanilla and process until just combined, 5 to 10 seconds. Scrape down the sides of the bowl, then add the lukewarm melted chocolate and pulse until smooth and creamy, 10 to 15 seconds. Do not overmix.

6. When the cakes have cooled, place one cake layer on a serving plate. Using an icing spatula or butter knife, spread about ¾ cup [200 g] of the frosting over the first layer. Top with the second layer, then spread the remaining frosting over the top and sides of the cake, swirling decoratively.

MAKE AHEAD: The cake can be made, frosted, and stored in a cake dome 1 day ahead of time. The frosting can be used immediately or held at room temperature for 3 to 4 hours. It may lose its shine as it sits—to fix it, run a metal spoon under hot water and wipe dry with a towel; stir the frosting with the hot spoon and it should shine right up.

pro tip

When melting chocolate, take care not to let it get too hot or it will "seize" and become unusable. I prefer to melt chocolate in the microwave in short intervals, but it can also be done in a double boiler on the stovetop. Either way, remove the chocolate from the heat before it is completely melted, letting the residual heat in the bowl or pan melt it completely.

Meatloaf Serves 4-6

3
2 T olive oil 4 Tbs. min

1 small onion, chopped
3 garlic cloves, minced
1 carrot, chopped
1 stalk celery, chopped
2 eggs (large)
(1/4 cup chopped parsley)
1 teaspoon salt (1 1/2 ?)
1/2 teaspoon pepper
1 T Worcestershire
2 lbs meatloaf mix 85?
2/3 cup bread crumbs
_____ sauce
(_ more)
_____
cream
_ lightly beaten
1 tsp dried oregano, salt
pepper

heat olive oil in 3-liter enameled skillet
add onions & garlic & cook over mod. heat
stirring freq. for 7-8 min until soft
but not brown. Stir in _____ & cook, stirring
constantly for 3-4 min. When all moisture
In heavy _____
over mod heat. T_____ milk
heat & stir in flour. Pour

creating recipes

The first original recipe I ever came up with was a saffron crepe soufflé with lump crabmeat and chives. Sounds fancy, right? It was for my final exam in culinary school, which entailed developing a recipe using classic French technique and demonstrating it in front of the entire class. I received an A on the recipe portion of the exam, but a C on the cooking demo. Public speaking was not my forté, and trying to do it while cooking was, well, let's just say there were a lot of awkward lulls in the presentation!

Thankfully, I quickly got over that humiliation and, all these years and hundreds of recipes later, creating recipes is still my passion. Sure, I often cook off the cuff, but there's something about a good, solid recipe that greatly appeals to me. If I'm going to spend time cooking, I like to know that a dish is going to come out perfectly every single time. And I like to guarantee that as much as I possibly can for my readers.

People often ask me where I get my inspiration for new recipes and how I create them. With food, there is never a shortage of ideas. I'm inspired by restaurant meals, travel, cookbooks, suggestions from readers and friends, the seasons, you name it.

Once I have an idea for a recipe, I thoroughly research it. Then I consider how I might alter the basic formula to suit my cooking style. Every dish has endless variations, and each chef or recipe developer can put their own spin on it. For example, I don't use hard-to-find ingredients in my recipes. Can I make substitutions? I don't typically make multi-step, time-consuming dishes. Are there store-bought products that can be used to save time? I like to give specific measurements for salt. How much is needed? I like food with bold flavor. Can I add another layer of flavor or intensify the seasoning? I like recipes that appeal to the whole family. How can I make it more kid-friendly?

Oftentimes, in coming up with new recipes, I rely on base recipes that I've developed over the years that are easily adaptable. For example, if a cherry scone catches my eye in a bakery, I'll use my basic cream scone recipe as a starting point, and then create a new recipe from there. There are always tweaks: cherries release juice, so I might have to increase the flour; cherries are also quite tart, so a little additional sugar might be called for; orange complements cherry, so maybe a bit of orange zest is added, and so on.

I write the recipe based on my assumptions before I ever start cooking. And then I hit the kitchen to test my theories. Sometimes I nail a dish on the first try; other times, it takes me multiple attempts and an entire week to get it right.

Once I have a dish perfected, I make it again to be sure it's foolproof. And then, finally, I ask myself the same two questions: "If I owned a restaurant or bakery, would I put this dish on the menu?" and "Am I excited to share this recipe with my readers?" If the answer is yes to both, it's a success!

cocktails

I can close my eyes and almost relive the nightly cocktail hour ritual at my grandparents' house, where I spent my childhood summers. Every evening at 6 o'clock, my grandfather would come upstairs from his basement office and pour himself a gin and tonic. Then, he'd mix drinks for my grandmother, my parents, and any friends who stopped by. I can still see all the adults sitting on the screened-in porch, chatting with drinks in hand, while my sister and I played on the tire swing that hung on the oak tree in the backyard.

Times have certainly changed—our "cocktail hour" is usually spent driving carpool sans cocktails—but we still find occasions to kick back and enjoy fun drinks now and then. The recipes in this chapter include some of my favorites for entertaining, like Sparkling White Sangria (page 283) or Pink Vodka Lemonade (page 284), both pitcher drinks that can be made ahead of time in large batches. There are also a few after-dinner surprises, like White Russian Milk Shakes (page 291) and Boozy Hot Chocolate (page 292)—which are basically cocktails as dessert. Cheers!

sparkling white sangria with nectarines, oranges & frozen grapes

WHENEVER WE VISIT my parents in Florida, we have dinner at Columbia, a Spanish/Cuban-style restaurant on Sarasota's St. Armands Circle. Mike and I always share a pitcher of their sparkling white sangria, which the server prepares tableside for a little drama. I thought it'd be fun to make at home for friends, so I created this copycat recipe. There's no need to use an expensive sparkling wine. Buy something affordable, and buy a lot—no matter how much sangria I make, I always find myself back in the kitchen chopping fruit to make another batch. Serves 4 to 6 (makes about 2 qt [2 L])

2 Tbsp [30 ml] brandy

2 Tbsp [30 ml] orange liqueur, such as Grand Marnier

⅓ cup [65 g] superfine sugar

1 orange, halved

2 limes

1 small apple, such as Fuji or Honeycrisp, peeled, cored and chopped

1 nectarine, chopped

1 bottle [750 ml] chilled sparkling wine, such as Cava, Prosecco, or Champagne

1 cup [240 ml] lemon-lime soda

A few bunches frozen grapes, for serving

Ice cubes, for serving

1. In a large pitcher, combine the brandy, orange liqueur, and sugar. Squeeze the juice from one orange half and one lime into the pitcher. Stir until the sugar dissolves. Slice the remaining orange half and lime into thin slices and add to the pitcher, then add the chopped apple and nectarine.

2. Add the sparkling wine, lemon-lime soda, and a large bunch of frozen grapes. Place ice cubes in glasses (do not put them in the pitcher or they'll water the drink down), along with small bunches of frozen grapes, and then pour the sangria over the top. Spoon some of the chopped fruit into the glasses and serve.

pro tip

Chill the sangria with frozen grapes. They look beautiful and won't water the drink down.

pink vodka lemonade

I LIKE TO HAVE A pitcher of drinks ready when guests arrive for a party. It gets things off to a fun start—plus, who wants to play bartender when you're mingling with friends and putting the finishing touches on a meal? This pink-alicious thirst quencher is perfect for a summertime girls' night in, bridal or baby shower, or any other girly get-together. The pretty color comes from puréed fresh strawberries. For a nonalcoholic version, you can replace the vodka with 2 cups of water. Serves 4 to 6 (makes about 1¾ qt [1.7 L])

½ lb [230 g] strawberries, trimmed and halved	1 cup [200 g] sugar, plus more to taste
1¾ cups [420 ml] fresh lemon juice, from 6 to 8 large lemons	1 cup [240 ml] lemon-flavored or regular vodka, plus more to taste
3 cups [720 ml] cold water	Ice cubes, for serving

pro tip

If you have a Vitamix blender, you can skip the step of straining the seeds.

1. In a blender, combine the strawberries and ½ cup [120 ml] of the lemon juice; purée until smooth, then force the mixture through a fine-mesh sieve into a large bowl to strain out the seeds. (The fastest way to force it through is by pressing a ladle in a circular motion against the sieve.) Transfer the mixture to a clean blender, then add the remaining 1¼ cups [300 ml] lemon juice, the cold water, the sugar, and the vodka and blend until the sugar is dissolved. Taste, then and add more sugar and vodka, if desired. Pour into glasses with ice cubes and serve.

kir royale

ONE OF THE FIRST THINGS I did after I landed in Paris as a college exchange student was enjoy a Kir Royale with friends at a sidewalk café in the bustling Latin Quarter. I was tipsy by lunchtime, and instantly head-over-heels *in love* with Paris.

A Kir Royale is a swanky aperitif made from Champagne and crème de cassis, a viscous black currant liqueur. (When the drink is made with still wine instead of Champagne, it's simply called a Kir.) For a bit of fun, I like to top the drinks with fresh raspberries, which float like festive little ice cubes. This is a great signature drink for a holiday party. Makes one 6½-oz [195-ml] cocktail

1 Tbsp [15 ml] crème de cassis or Chambord

6 oz [180 ml] cold dry Champagne

A few raspberries, for garnish

sourcing savvy

Feel free to substitute any sparkling wine for the Champagne.

1. Pour the crème de cassis into a champagne flute, then add the Champagne. Top off with a few fresh raspberries.

mojito jelly shots

heads up

Allow several hours for the gelatin in these shots to set up.

DID YOU EVER THINK you'd find a jelly-shot recipe in this book? I know, me neither! Admittedly, until making these, I had never even tried a jelly shot. I found the original recipe in *Food & Wine* from Chef Michael Symon years ago, and curiosity got the best of me. Made from real mojito ingredients—like fresh mint, lime, and rum—they are a sophisticated version of those Dixie-cup concoctions from your college days. Such fun for a party! Makes about 30 shots

sourcing savvy

You can find plastic shot cups at party stores or order them online; just be sure to get the kind with lids so that they are easy to transport to a party.

1½ cups [360 ml] water

1 cup [200 g] sugar

3 envelopes (¾ oz [20 g]) unflavored gelatin

1 cup [240 ml] fresh lime juice, from 8 to 10 limes

1 cup [20 g] tightly packed fresh mint leaves

1 cup [240 ml] coconut-flavored rum, such as Malibu (white rum may be substituted)

1. In a small saucepan, bring the water and sugar to a gentle boil. Stir until the sugar dissolves, a few minutes. Gradually sprinkle the gelatin over the sugar water, whisking constantly over low heat until the gelatin is completely dissolved, about 1 minute. Off the heat, add the lime juice and mint leaves to the pan and let steep for 15 minutes.

2. Stir in the rum, then strain the mixture through a fine-mesh sieve into a bowl that has a pouring spout or a 1-qt [1-L] liquid measuring cup, pressing on the mint leaves with the back of a spoon to extract as much liquid as possible.

3. Arrange 30 small plastic cups on a large rimmed baking sheet. Pour the mojito mixture into the cups, and then refrigerate until firm, 2 to 3 hours.

4. The gelatin will stick to the cups, making it difficult to get out. Before serving, either run the bottom of each cup under very warm water until the gelatin melts just slightly around the edges, or pour some warm (not hot) water into the rimmed baking sheet and let the shots sit until the warmth of the water melts the gelatin just slightly around the edges. Either method will allow the shot to slide easily out of the cup; if you go with the second method, be extra careful not to leave the shots in warm water too long, or they'll completely melt (in which case, all is not lost—you can always put them back in the fridge to firm up). Serve immediately with toothpicks or mini plastic spoons.

white russian milk shakes

A WHITE RUSSIAN IS A decadent after-dinner cocktail made from vodka, sweet coffee liqueur, and heavy cream, served on ice. Since a White Russian is basically a dessert (that gets you buzzed), I figured, "Why not take it one step further and transform it into a milk shake?" My friends go crazy for these—and a dollop of whipped cream on top doesn't hurt, either. Serves 2

¼ cup [60 ml] vodka

¼ cup [60 ml] Kahlúa

1 qt [960 ml] best-quality vanilla ice cream

Cocoa powder, chocolate shavings, and/or Sweetened Whipped Cream (page 292), for topping (optional)

1. In a blender, combine the vodka, Kahlúa, and ice cream and purée until smooth and creamy. Pour into glasses, then dust with cocoa powder and/or sprinkle with chocolate shavings. Serve immediately, with whipped cream, if desired.

boozy hot chocolate

MADE WITH REAL CHOCOLATE, this cozy concoction is like drinking a creamy, boozy milk chocolate bar. Sometimes I give the recipe a Mexican twist by adding a dash of cinnamon and a pinch of cayenne pepper and replacing the whiskey with tequila. You can also omit the booze to make it kid-friendly—although, consider yourself warned: the kids won't want the easy powdered cocoa mix after tasting this! Serves 4 to 6

1 qt [1 L] whole milk

1 cup [240 ml] heavy cream

¼ cup [55 g] packed dark brown sugar

1 Tbsp natural unsweetened cocoa powder

Pinch of salt

8 oz [230 g] bittersweet chocolate, roughly chopped

½ tsp vanilla extract

Whiskey or bourbon, for serving (rum or tequila may be substituted)

Sweetened Whipped Cream, for serving (recipe follows)

1. In a medium saucepan, whisk together the milk, cream, brown sugar, cocoa powder, and salt over high heat. Bring to a simmer. Remove from the heat; add the chocolate and vanilla and whisk until the chocolate is melted. Ladle into mugs and top each drink with 2 tablespoons whiskey or bourbon, or the desired amount, and whipped cream, if desired.

sweetened whipped cream

½ cup [120 ml] heavy cream

1 Tbsp confectioners' sugar

¼ tsp vanilla extract

1. In a cold medium bowl, whip the cream with a whisk until slightly thickened. Add the confectioners' sugar and vanilla and continue whipping until the cream holds its shape.

how to stock a home bar

I created my first home bar when my children were young because going out to restaurants suddenly became a major operation—and babysitters made it costly. Entertaining at home was much more relaxing. And if you have friends over on a Saturday night and you're hiding your children upstairs, you definitely have to offer those friends a drink!

You don't need to be an expert bartender to be a great host—you just need the know-how and ingredients to make a few classic cocktails. And if you're just starting out, don't feel like you have to stock your liquor cabinet in one fell swoop. Most classic drinks are made just from a handful of hard liquors or spirits—namely gin, vodka, tequila, rum, and whiskey—so it's best to start with those and build from there. Once you've got the basics, you can gradually add secondary ingredients, such as liqueurs, fortified wines, and mixers to your collection.

Liqueurs (not to be confused with hard liquors) are spirits that have been sweetened and flavored with fruit, cream, herbs, spices, flowers, or nuts. Think: Cointreau, Amaretto, Baileys Irish Cream, Campari, Frangelico, St-Germain, Kahlúa, and Sambuca. Fortified wines, such as Port, Sherry, Madeira, Marsala, and Vermouth, are wines to which a hard liquor is added. And, finally, mixers are nonalcoholic ingredients added to cocktails, such as soda, tonic water, fruit juice, and egg whites.

With the essential hard liquors in your home bar, you can shop for liqueurs, fortified wines, and mixers one party/cocktail at a time. For example, if you're planning to serve margaritas with Mexican food for a get-together, supplement your tequila with Cointreau and fresh limes. If you want to make dirty vodka martinis for a cocktail party, buy a bottle of dry Vermouth and a jar of olives. If boozy after-dinner coffee is on the menu, pick up a bottle of Baileys or Kahlúa. After a while, you'll have a well-stocked bar with ingredients to make any number of popular cocktails. And don't just think of your home bar in terms of drinks; alcohol adds wonderful depth of flavor to many recipes.

Another reason to stock your bar slowly is that alcohol can be expensive. In most liquor stores, the choices are seemingly limitless, and the prices range from reasonable to "Yikes!" You want to select good to premium brands based on the cocktails you're planning to make. For example, if you're drinking whiskey neat (without mixers or ice), splurge on a quality bottle since the whiskey is the star of the show. But opt for a mid-priced rum if you're planning on mixing it with simple syrup and lime juice for daiquiris. Another way to save money is to buy liqueurs in mini bottles. They're used in much smaller quantities than hard liquors and they go a long way.

To complete your bar, you'll need a few essential bar tools: a cocktail shaker, a mixing glass, a jigger (or mini liquid measuring cup), a citrus juicer or reamer, a Hawthorne strainer, a muddler, a bar spoon, cocktail picks, a vegetable peeler, and ice cube trays. And lastly, you'll need a good cocktail recipe book.

Cheers!

with gratitude

It takes a village to write a cookbook! This book would not have been possible without the help of my wonderful recipe testers, who gave of their time so generously to ensure every recipe was thoroughly tested and perfected.

Priscilla Acosta
Emilie Ahern
Carol Ahrens
Jackie Ajazi
Liz Albert
Mary Ann Alcon
Kathy Allen
Ronda Allen
Jean Anderson
Jo Andrews
Fran Antolina Bickel
Sandy Appl
Valerie April
Lisa Arends
Sandra Armando
Joan Asinas
Mary Bach
Pat Baker
Mary Ellen Barry
Marianne Beardall
Karen Beckman
Jennifer Becksvoort
Amy Berryhill
Wendy Beseda
Lora Bevirt
Fran Bickel
Robyn Blond
John Bobin
Lindsay Boller
Kelli Bordessa
Mary Bordoni
Dawn Bourdo
Kitty Bower
Jackie Brence
Kristen Brodrick
Elaine Brown
Donna M. Browne
Judy Browning
Carole Bruno
Peggy Burelli
Diana Burke
Linda Buschman
Diane Butler
Marlene Butler
Sue Canvasser
Kimberly Carmichael

Julie Cary
Hope Cassano
Caroline Castillo
Shannon Chang
Patt Chase
Melinda Chen
Weiwen Chen
Debbie Chiet
Vivian Chiu
Julie Christiansen
Susan Clayman
Peggy Clayton Kirk
Janet Cohen
Kim Cohen
Terry Cohler
Jeanette Colon
Kitty Connor
Alison Cooper
Mary Heston Cooper
Jane Cooper-Kelly
Barbara Copes
Anne Cordes
Linda Corsetti
Angela Coscio
Tim Crawford
Dani Crichton
Carrie Crockett
Carl Crowe
Melanie Csellak
Linda G. Darling
Sally Darling
Cristie Dasher
Alice Davis
Sandra de Helen
Danni Dean
Hedy DeCampo
Amy Decker
Lindy Deckert
Deb Degnan
Lorie DeMarcay
Ann-Marie DeRosa
Cindy DeVries
Kristen Dhillon
Judee Diehl
Wakako Dillon
Laura Dinh

Susan Disidore
Susan Dobrowney
Sara Dolan
Sue Downes
Sandy Drechsel
Nancy Dressel
Charlene Driggs
Robin Duncan
Kristina Dunn
Debra Duplak
Carley Dyer
Gia Elsevier
Deb Endyke
Michelle Engmann
Monica Evans
Cristina Everett
Constance Felten
Donna Toutjian Fletcher
Barbara Flores
Robbie Foxx
Carol Frampton
Vicki Frederick
Connie Fritsch
Kerianne Frylinck
Rika Fujimoto
Sarah Fulytar
Susanna Alcaro Funk
Kathie Galloway
Joe Gannon
Tracy Ganti
Linda Geen
Julie Geffre
Jan Gessin
Karen Gilpin
Katya Gimbel
Tamera Gjesdal
Wendy Glasser
Cathie Glowa
Jordan Goldsmith
Grant Goodner
Allison Grasso
Denise Graves
Jacqueline Griffin
Linda Grimes
Reyanne Guerrero
Hiromi Gupta

Mindy Halpern
Bonnie Handel
Barbara Hanson
Terry Hare
Shaleyna Harper
Jennett Harrell
Ruth Harris
Ellen Harrison
Jennifer Hart
Peggy Haser
Eileen Haynes
Kristen He
Kathie Heli
Lynn Heron
Grace Hetherington
Jane Hiemstra
Cyndi Hilton-Geary
Tammy Hines
Nanci Hirschorn
Hazel Hodgkins
Christine Hoeksema
Beth Hoffman
Connie Hoffman
Tammy Hondo
Mary Howell
Carol Humphreys
Belinda Hunter
Kim Hurren
Jane Ingalls
Karen Ivanis-Rogers
Laurie Ivy
Jill Jachimek
Rebecca Jackson
Deborah Jacobs
Laurie Jamieson
Daryn Janis
Lashana Johnson
Sue Jones
Gay Judson
Dana Kaminsky
Lynn Kaniss
Laura Kargov
Patti Kiernan
Bev Kloppenburg
Sherry Klusman
Barbara Knoll

Pam Koepf
Wendy Krakower
Debra Kraus
Beverly Krikorian
Connie Krueger
Nicole Kustner
Anna Lacy
Natalie Lalka
Connie Landwehr
Deb Lang
Tricia Larkin
Nancy Law
Jan Leeth
Marianne Lehman
Lorraine Lepler
Kristin LeQuier
Tabitha Lichty
Kathy Liebmann
Michele Lillie
Nancy Lipford
Angie Lofgreen
Esty Lohnberg
Serena Lok
Elan Long
Grace Long
Mary Loseby
Meredith Loveless
Helene & David Lowry
Cindy Lucarotti
Linda Luce
Robin MacGillivray
Laura Mancini
Lisa Manning
Jennifer Marcus
Christina Martin
Lesley Martin
Isabel Mateus
Cheryl Mathias
Michelle Matson
Kate Matthews
Amanda Maultsby
Mary Ellen Maynard
Cae McCreary
Juliane McDavid
Emilie McGee
Suzzy McLean
Alicia McLelland
Gail McMullen
Patti Merlo
Barbara Miciul
Judy Mikula
Karen Miner
Pamela L. Minkley

Pamela Minkley
Pilar Montalvo
Maria Morelli
Donna Morse
Cassie Moses
Amy Mroch
Mary Munson
Jack Murphy
Janise Brown Murphy
Becky Musta
Nathan Nangia
Jo Ann Natt
Linda G. Natt
Ronnie Neufeld Oliver
Caroline Ng
Dejana Nikitovic
Dana Niven
Angela Nogueira
Gail Nottenburg
Diana Oertli
Gayann Oneal
Donna Ordille
Jim Orvis
Barbara Osborn
Corinne Osborne
David Ostrowski
Carolyn Owsley
Mona Pafford
Wendy Paler
Brooke Palmer
Dori Panagis
Ker-Yng Pang
Jeanne Paschal
Barbara Patterson
Marcy Patterson
Lauren Paul
Dale Paulshock
Nancy Soldi Peckham
Linda Perrin
Meghan Pillow
Celeste & Beatrice Pocher
Debbie Pollack
Elizabeth Prest
Jan Prows
Barbara Purtill
Erin Putnam
Cheryl Quattrini
Joy Rabbini
Janice Ramirez
Suzan Reed
Linda Reid
Mary Reiling
Valerie Reiske

Germaine Rekwest
Linda Remick
Cherie Remmer
Beth Renzetti
Diana Reyes Suderman
Nikki Reynolds
Susie Rings
Kim Rippere
Susan Rittenberg
Barbara Rizzolo
Claire Roberts
Maria Roberts
Susan Rocco
Sherri Roda
Julie Roedell
Michelle Rogers
Elizabeth Rose
Nancy Rose
Robin Rosner
Roberta Roth
Anne Rubin
Veronica Rubin
Shayna Rudick
Shirley Ruszkowski
Karen Sabbath
Tracy Santoro
Sandra Scherer
Karen Schillinger
Jean Schloss
Lucienne Schmidt
Nancy Schneider
Stephanie Sears
Lauri Selib
Margot Selig
Harriet Shanzer
Sue Shortley
Joan Shuler
Malea Siemens
Birgitte Simen
Elisa Skadahl
Lisa Sletmoe
Karen & David Smith
Pam Soule
Chuck Spangler
Shani Spiegle
Faye Stafiej
Trish Stapleton
Frank Starks
Brenda Stepp
Mike Stines, Ph.B.
Christina Stone
Liz Sullivan
Sue Swan

Nisha Tailor
William Tate
Mary Tawasha
Shauna Taylor
Brenda Y. Terrell
Jason Tevnan
Sally Theran
Ellen Thomas
Julie Thompson
Maria Tina
Janice Topf Shankman
Pat Trehy
Katherine Triest
Arielle Troiano
Jan Troy
Debbie Tucker
Cynthia Turner
David, Deb &
    Charlotte Usprich
Sarah Van Wagner
Dena Veerasammy
Tony Vendely
Jane Volk-Brew
Margo Waite
Kristen Wallace
Renee Watts
Hope Weinman
Christy Weintraub
Jill Weisensee
Kathy Westlund
Karen Whritenour
Lynn Wiegand
Lorna Wiens
Minnie Wilkes
Mary Willman
Ashlea Wilson
Johnese Wilson
Debbie Winick
Helene Winschel
Rickie Wise
Amy Wollins
Lynne Wong
Randi Wortman
Susan Wright
Caroline Yaun
Lana Yee
Abner Yong
Ann Yoshihashi
Heidi Youngs
Harriet Zaidman

index